CONSIDER

Lew Weider & Ben Gutierrez

Permissions Department
Academx Publishing Services, Inc.

P.O. Box 56527
Virginia Beach, VA 23456
Printed in the United States of America

ISBN-10: 1-60036-424-1
ISBN-13: 978-1-60036-424-2

To the exceptional students of Liberty University—

You sharpen our thinking with your valuable insights,

You energize us with your enthusiasm for life,

You humble us by your commitment to Christ.

You are the finest students in the world!

There is no better place to teach than at Liberty University!

ACKNOWLEDGMENTS

This page serves to recognize the myriad of support we received in writing this book. Without their help, we would not have been able to complete this very satisfying task.

Thank you to our wives Cheryl Weider and Tammy Gutierrez, whose support and encouragement through the ups and downs of life keep us going and enthused to continue to minister.

Thank you to our precious children, Crystal and Zach Beams, Michelle Weider, Lauren Ashton Gutierrez, and Emma Jordan Gutierrez. You fill our lives with such joy and laughter. Our prayer is that every day we will live out before you the truths taught in this book. We love you so much.

To Jill Walker, your acute attention to detail in managing the editing process of this book has been unparalleled. Your professionalism, knowledge of the process, and flexible spirit have been the most critical factors in finishing this book. Without your contribution, this book couldn't have been completed. Many thanks!

To Anne Alexander, thank you for paying attention to the smallest of details. Your technical editing improved the overall readability of the book and added the finishing touches to the manuscript. Anne can be contacted for writing and editing projects through WordWise, LLC at annea2@bellsouth.net.

To our leadership and colleagues of Liberty University, thank you for your encouragement to write, teach, administrate, lead, and dream big. You provide us with the richest environments within which to edify the Body of Christ. There is no better place to live, work, and minister than Liberty Mountain!

TABLE OF CONTENTS

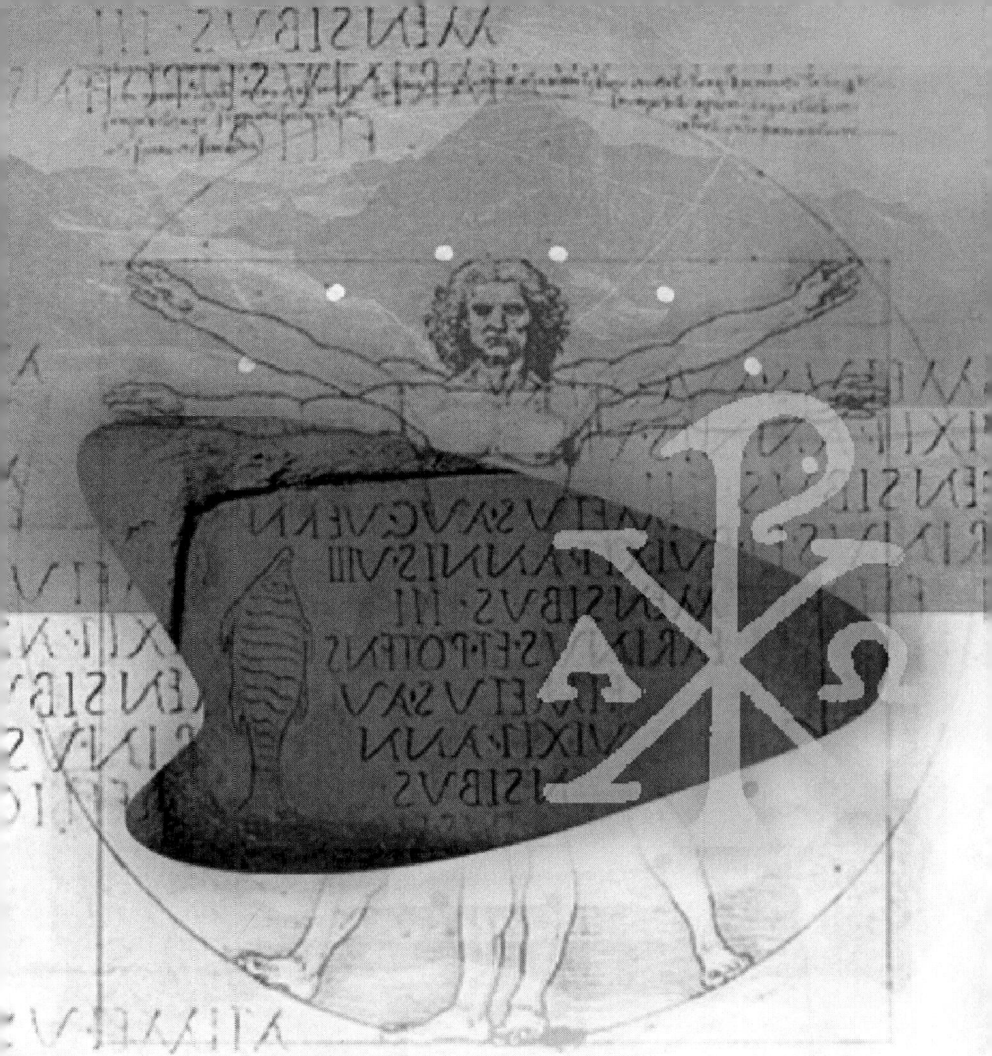

INTRODUCTION

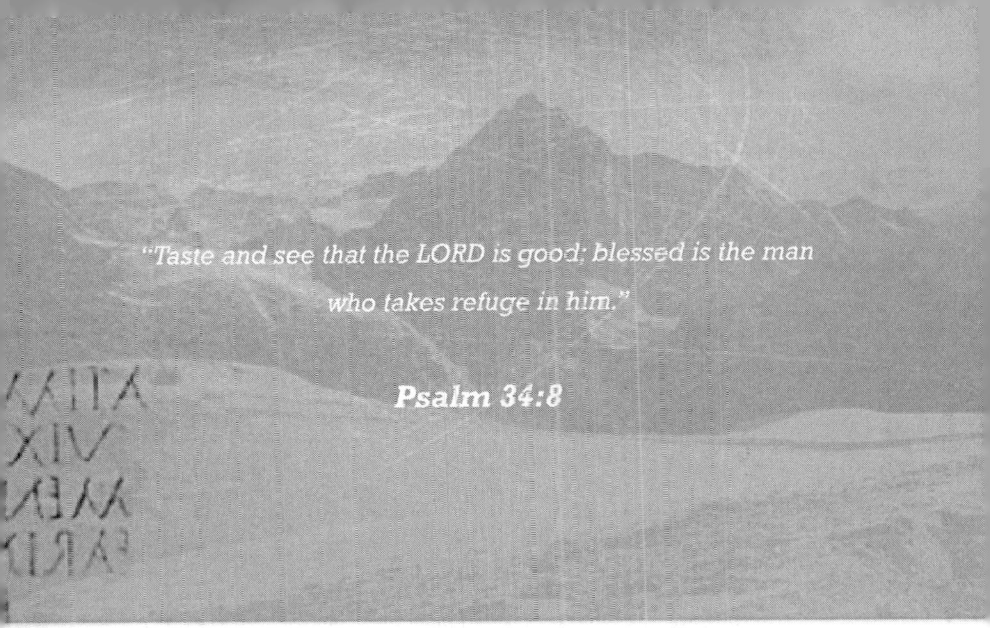

"Taste and see that the LORD is good; blessed is the man who takes refuge in him."

Psalm 34:8

THE JOURNEY BEGINS

YOU WILL NEVER FORGET THIS.

"Hang on!" You are about to begin a journey of a lifetime. Beginning today you are embarking on a journey that has the potential to change your life forever. While on this journey, you will contemplate thoughts and ideas that will profoundly stimulate both your heart and mind. You will be asked to ponder profound concepts and realities that will remain etched in your mind for many years to follow. Hopefully what you experience in the coming days will positively change your life forever and provide you with fond memories that will last a lifetime.

WE'RE ALL IN THIS TOGETHER.

We desire nothing more than to walk this journey with you. So, don't worry if you begin to feel unsure about what you might have believed to be true all your life. Because we too have asked ourselves the tough questions about life, death, eternity, and our purpose in this world. Collectively, we have talked to hundreds of students who have asked of us the same kind of questions. You are not alone in your quest for answers. You are studying alongside many of us who have grappled with the same questions. And just as we appreciated a patient, listening ear with which to process these thoughts, we trust you will be surrounded with patient and willing people who will encourage and support you as you process the truths and realities that are presented here.

LET'S TALK.

This book is intended to be an extension of the many conversations that we have had with friends, family members, students, colleagues, and parishioners over the years. We have found that some are closer than others in coming to their own conclusions about these things. And even those who have told us that they have already made their decision as to what to believe about life, death, eternity and their purpose in this world, we still relish the opportunity to help them further process and clarify their beliefs. Regardless of who we talk to about these issues, our preference is to have a calm, relaxed and courteous conversation with anyone who is willing to engage in a rational dialogue. And usually it is hovered around a fresh pot of French-press coffee at our favorite coffee shop (the bolder the better)!

YOU WILL BE RESPECTED.

We have purposed to write this book in a non-shaming, non-abrasive manner. We believe that people can discuss profound, life-impacting truths about life while maintaining a courteous and respectful attitude to all who may still be processing the truths of Christianity. Therefore, we have made every attempt to display the sincerest respect to those who have not yet placed their faith in Jesus Christ as their Lord and Savior. It is our goal to present what we believe as truth without imposing any blame or guilt or shame. Please accept our heartfelt apologies if you feel that any portion of this book presents the truth in a disrespectful manner.

THERE'S NO HIDING OUR PASSION.

Still, it will not take you too long to notice that we are passionate about the subject we are discussing, and we feel a deep sense of love and urgency for all to "taste and see that the Lord is good" (Psalm 34:8a). We won't masquerade our earnest desire for our readers to logically process the information and ultimately make a rational, personal decision to believe that Jesus Christ is God who came to earth to provide the only way of salvation. But what we believe to be true will be sincerely and respectfully presented for discussion. We cannot alter nor suppress the evident conclusions and requirements that truth may make upon our lives – that will be a personal point of decision for each of us. But our hope is that we have done nothing to distract you from hearing and receiving the pure and simple truth about Jesus Christ.

IT'S NOT ABOUT US.

We're not perfect—far from it. In fact, we believe it is the height of arrogance to claim that we – in and of ourselves – have all the answers. We are quick to recommend that you investigate other books from Christian authors who may elaborate further on the concepts you will read about in this book. No pride here. We recognize that certain authors resonate with you better than others, so we encourage you to continue to seek the truth found in the Scriptures from other reliable sources. We ultimately believe there is only one unparalleled, infallible source of truth and one God the Father and one Savior, Jesus Christ. We also have discovered that it is helpful to process these truths with others who have studied the Bible and have an effective way to explain difficult topics.

JUST ENOUGH.

Even though there are some very intriguing questions that will be left unanswered in this book, we believe that you will have enough information with which to make the most profound decision of your lives – to place your faith and hope in Jesus Christ to be the forgiver and Savior of your souls and the restorer of true peace in your lives.

WE'LL WALK WITH YOU.

Even though we hope you will feel a great sense of urgency to come to a point of personal faith and devotion to Jesus Christ, we will make a solemn pledge to walk with you on this spiritual journey for as long as it takes. It may take some time for you to consider how this truth will impact your own life and that's OK. So, we will adopt the position that the Apostle Paul set for all of us who have the responsibility to teach others – to do so with "patience" (2 Timothy 4:2b). But never forget that, "now is the time of God's favor, now is the day of salvation" (2 Corinthians 6:2).

WE'LL COMMIT.

We understand that there is no way we could possibly meet each and every person that reads this book, but we will promise to pray for you regularly and ask God to grant you the time and energy to give serious thought to the truths that we will discuss in the coming days. We will pray that you will not only learn facts about God, but that you will come to know Him personally as your loving Heavenly Father, a Father who loves you unconditionally.

OUR PRAYER FOR YOU...

As we begin this life-changing journey, we offer this prayer to God on your behalf:

Dear God,

Today, we begin a journey that some may have never traveled before. For today, we are really giving serious thought about spiritual matters and how You relate to us and how we should relate to You.

I know, for some this will be brand new – for some, uncomfortable – still others will feel apprehensive. Please, Lord, would You give us the wisdom to listen and respectfully contemplate the truth about You?

For each and every student who is found reading this book right now, would You please bring them one step closer to You today?

For some, would You excite them about the truth of Jesus Christ – assuring them that their faith in You is sound and secure?

For others, would You surprise them with the truth about Jesus Christ so that they will accept You as the Lord and Savior of their soul?

For still others, would You grant them the freedom in their souls to sincerely contemplate and ponder what they read in order to consider the teachings of You in a fair and respectful manner?

And at the end, may each and every one of us gain a deeper appreciation of who You are and sincerely value YOU! And amid our admiration of You, we pray that everyone would accept You as their needed Savior and Redeemer of their souls.

May all who read this book, "Taste and see that the LORD is good; blessed is the man who takes refuge in him." (Psalm 34:8)

Amen.

—Lew Weider & Ben Gutierrez

CHAPTER ONE

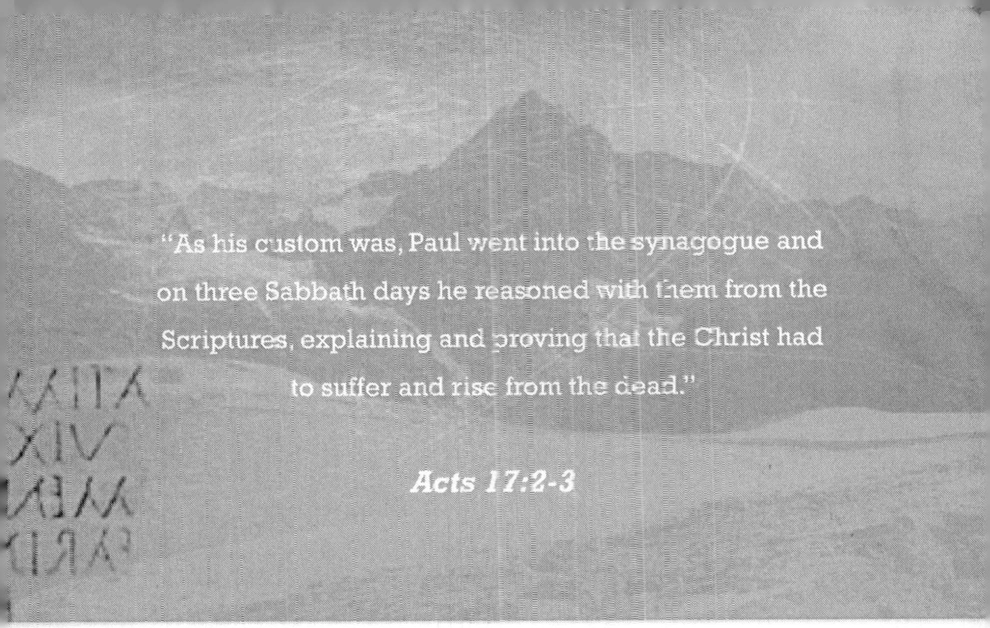

"As his custom was, Paul went into the synagogue and on three Sabbath days he reasoned with them from the Scriptures, explaining and proving that the Christ had to suffer and rise from the dead."

Acts 17:2-3

A CALL TO CONSIDER

"Consider what?!" – "I've never heard this before!" – "Let's talk later." "Forget it." – "Don't call me, I'll call you." – "I see the logic." – "Tell me more." "I get it now!" – "I believe."

DON'T BE SURPRISED

You too will experience these very diverse reactions when you discuss matters of life and spirituality. Whether you are talking to friends, family, coworkers, or strangers, when you ask others to consider unfamiliar spiritual concepts, you will inevitably experience similar responses. But the reassuring thing is that you are not alone in experiencing this diversity of reactions. Many before you have experienced these very same reactions on a daily basis, and they have responded appropriately. Fortunately, we have their example to follow.

One of the greatest theologians and scholars in history experienced every one of these responses. In fact, these kinds of responses became common place for him. After every lecture or discussion that the Apostle Paul had with people concerning the person of Jesus, he faced a diversity of reactions from his audience. If Paul addressed the fact that God came to earth in the form of a baby (Jesus), there was skepticism. Or if the Apostle talked about how this God-man (Jesus) lived a perfect sinless life and then offered His own life as a sacrificial payment for the sin of all mankind, Paul was run out of town. If he addressed the issue of how Jesus literally rose again from the grave to prove that He had authority and power to save every person's soul, the aftermath was unpredictable. The Apostle Paul just stood back and braced for the inevitable reaction – a chaotic swell of diverse emotion.

In a word, the Apostle Paul often witnessed a display of emotional "chaos."
Some believed.
Others did not.
Some treated him with respect.
Others abrasively and rudely shouted at him.
Some scheduled an appointment to talk to him later.
Others attempted to literally kill him.

WHY THE DIVERSITY?

Simply put, people react differently because everybody is created differently. Every human being is unique. Not one of us has the same fingerprints. Some differences are subtly recognizable while some differences are obvious and overt. Because we are all wired differently, people will undoubtedly react differently to questions that are posed to them. In fact, our diversity in personality should testify of the unspeakable power and beauty of God in the act and art of creating us.

And if you want to see one of the most vivid and unbridled exhibitions of diversity of emotion, just try asking a group of people to consider changing a lifelong belief, something that they had regarded to be true for all their lives. Then ask them to consider an idea that would utterly and completely alter their lives forever. Make sure you stand back at a safe distance, because you're about to see some major sparks fly.

Paul knew this was the inclination of many who would be asked to consider spiritual truth for the first time. He understood this would occur because he took his lead from another prominent historical person that experienced the most visceral exhibition of hatred from people but maintained a sincere love for them. This model example for the Apostle Paul (and us) was Jesus Christ.

CASE IN POINT

Jesus showed and taught His followers how to expect the unexpected when talking about spiritual issues. One notable day, Jesus traveled to an extremely diverse land called the Decapolis region. There He encountered a man so unspeakably different from the rest of his countrymen that they ostracized him to the outskirts of their land. As a result, this man took his residence amid a graveyard near the coast of the Sea of Galilee. As one approached the beach head, this man could be heard screaming at the top of his lungs day and night. He was reported to have been cutting himself unceasingly with the edges of stones. And it was not uncommon for him to exhibit an inhuman ability to break things in two that would have been impenetrable to others. This was the man Jesus intentionally desired to talk to about spiritual truths, truths that could change his life.

What was this frantic man's response? Emotional chaos. As soon as this man locked eyes with Jesus, he ran at full stride toward Jesus and His twelve disciples. The biblical account does not record what the disciples were thinking as they witnessed one of the most disturbed individuals start running at full speed towards them. I'm guessing they were freaking out! But what we do know is that Jesus remained calm. He looked past the chaos and patiently began to speak to this disturbed man.

What began in chaos ended in the man's life being utterly changed. In fact, he exhibited such tranquil behavior that the city's onlookers dropped what they were doing and ran to tell others about what had happened on the beachhead that day. But the story doesn't end here.

This man's chaotic-to-calm reaction to meeting Jesus Christ for the first time is actually not the reaction that is so unsettling to the reader. What is even more curious is how the people responded when they saw the miracle of this man's changed life. The diversity of their responses demonstrates the wide range of reactions when people are exposed to life-changing truth.

AN UNPREDICTED RESPONSE

After the townspeople personally observed the remarkable power of Jesus and how He singlehandedly changed the behavior of this crazy man, they immediately ran as fast as they could to tell their friends what had happened. They reported what they had witnessed firsthand, and they confirmed that Jesus had just fixed the number one social problem in their city. They testified of how Jesus not only got the man to stop screaming, but that Jesus was able to change the very countenance of this man—so much so that this man was no longer acting hostile and uncontrollable. He was now civil, calm, and desiring to learn more from the one who just changed his life. Immediately, the people from the city traveled to the place where they had ostracized this man in order to witness for themselves the colossal change that had taken place.

What do you think their reaction was to the amazing change in this man's life? Do you think they were so appreciative that Jesus solved their number one social problem that they would ask Him to go around and miraculously solve the other social problems they had in the city? Did they thank Jesus incessantly for doing what they were unable to do? How passionate do you think they were to try to persuade Jesus to stay? What was their response to this amazing incident?

As soon as they arrived at the beachhead, they saw the formerly crazy man sitting calmly, fully clothed, and in his right frame of mind. It was hard to believe it was the same man they had thrown outside the city walls and simply ignored. They had been powerless to do anything with him. This transformation was beyond their comprehension. In their bewilderment, they turned to Jesus and made an astounding demand.

"Leave."

"Leave!"

"Get out of here!"

"Get in your boat and never come back!"

Why did they react this way? Why did they choose to ostracize Jesus when Jesus was the one who healed the man they chose to ostracize? It seems like a backwards response, doesn't it? It makes no sense...or does it?

EXPECT THE UNEXPECTED

Even though we would not have anticipated this ending to the story, we are not surprised that they asked the one who delivered the truth to "get away." Experience has shown me that when someone encounters something that is so overwhelmingly powerful and/or something that would cause them to have to alter their fixed traditions or long-held beliefs, that person seems to need a little break from it all – just to let it sink in.

This story is found in the Gospel of Mark, Chapter Five, in the New Testament. It's interesting to note that the townspeople never denied that Jesus had a unique ability and power. Nor did they deny that Jesus totally changed the life of a man they were powerless to help. But what was both a miraculous and scary moment for them was also the moment when they were confronted with the Source of truth, Jesus.

They wondered what it all meant. They had just witnessed the evidence of Jesus' supernatural power, and they had questions. "Are we to learn something from this man? What does this say about our god(s)?" They had grown up thinking their gods were the most powerful of all. They concluded, "It's probably best to run this man out of town!" The whole experience was so new, so perplexing, so daunting. It was their watershed moment to question their own faith in what they held as truth. This moment caused them to consider Jesus' earth-shattering claims that flew at the very foundation of their theological and religious beliefs. And they needed time to process it all.

A LIFE WORTH FOLLOWING

So, did Jesus stay in their country? Did He insist that they hear Him out further? Did Jesus insist they stay and listen to His preaching so as not to lose the impact of this moment? No. He actually honored their request. He instructed His disciples to follow Him back to the boat, and they sailed away. Jesus understood that His departure would actually contribute to the process of those people coming to an understanding of Jesus' power, love, forgiveness, and ultimately to the salvation of their souls.

What is interesting is that as Jesus was getting into the boat, the man he had healed "begged to go with Him" (Mark 5:18). It sounds strange at first, but if you think about, it makes sense. This man who had been ignored for years finally found someone who cared for him as a person, someone who gave him the attention and love he had desired for a long time. But Jesus' reaction to his request was very unexpected. Jesus did not let him come along. As the story unfolds we find that Jesus had a good reason for His response.

Just as the testimony of Jesus and His disciples played a part in the process of making others notice truth, Jesus understood that this changed man would also play a part in the process of others hearing and understanding the truth. So, Jesus instructed this man to stay there. "Go home to your family and tell them how much the Lord has done for you, and how He has had mercy on you." And with this directive, Jesus and His disciples pushed the boat offshore and left a brand new believer in Jesus Christ on the shore with the hostile, unfriendly countrymen that he had lived with all his life.

Are you wondering whatever happened to this man and his country-men? Did they ever come to grips with their traditional religious ideologies that were totally devastated by Jesus' miracle? You will find the answer in Mark 7:31-8:10. Upon visiting this region for a second time, Jesus was met on the same beachhead by literally thousands of people who had come to hear His words and experience His teaching. Apparently the once disturbed man shared the story of his transformation with people all over the region. He was part of the process for thousands of people to come hear what Jesus had to say the next time He was in the area. Even today, if you travel to Israel, you can walk on the very same beachhead that many believe is the actual location where this miraculous event took place.

YOU MIGHT FIND YOURSELF IN THE SAME BOAT

Just as the previous incident took the people anywhere from one to two years before they came to a true faith in Jesus Christ as their Savior, likewise you might experience a similar time frame when you discuss spiritual things with those who are considering the validity of God's truth. It takes time to process truth, especially when that truth goes against all of one's pre-conceived ideas. And just like Jesus experienced, there will be times when you will want to stay and insist they listen to the life-changing truth that you want to share with them. But you, too, will possibly hear something like, "Leave." "Get out of here!" "Get in whatever brought you here and never come back!" And if that should happen, you need to honor the request, following Jesus' example. It just might be their watershed moment. Trust Jesus with the timing of the process for those to come to an understanding of truth.

ARE WE ANY DIFFERENT?

Whenever I (Ben) read this account in the Bible, I often wonder, "Are we any different today than those townspeople who did not want to acknowledge that Jesus is indeed the rightful authority of our lives?" You see, to adopt all the claims and truths of Jesus Christ, it implies that an authority is now in place above them which means they no longer hold veto power on all things in their life. Even though God should be their Lord and Savior, they trust themselves, first and foremost. Most of us do not want to relinquish our control and trust another to have an authoritative say in our lives—even when that authority is God Himself.

And when we talk to people, we need to help them process the truth so they will realize the wisdom in relinquishing their control and submitting to God. Until that realization is made, they will be like the townspeople on the beach and tell God to "Leave!"

Fortunately, God clearly provides instructions in the Bible for us to follow in order to help others process and understand biblical truth.

HOW WOULD YOU RESPOND?

And for some of us who desire to share the truth of Jesus Christ adequately helping people process the truth found in the Bible, how should we respond to similar responses of those who have yet to place their faith in Jesus Christ? There is a verse in the Bible that depicts what our reaction should be to those who offer any sort of objection when we ask them to consider our spiritual message:

"Preach the Word; be prepared in season and out of season; correct, rebuke and encourage – with great patience and careful instruction." (2 Timothy 4:2)

Three instructions come to us from this sentence in the Bible about how we ought to ask people to consider spiritual truth: Pleading. Precision. Patience.

BELIEVE WHAT YOU SAY

The Greek word translated "preach" in this translation is actually the first century word that means "to proclaim." It implies passion as produced by one's sincere belief in the spiritual message. This word can be used in a formal sense (as clergy "preach" on Sunday), or it can be used in an informal sense (as anyone can "proclaim" or "tell in order to make their point perfectly clear" to any listener.) Thus, it can apply to people in a church building hearing a sermon, or it can also apply to someone making their point clear as they discuss spiritual concepts while sitting casually on a park bench. Either way, anyone can "passionately preach the word." Therefore, if you desire to tell someone about how Jesus Christ can utterly change his/her life forever, they need to sense passion in your pleading. They ought to be totally convinced that you yourself believe what you are saying with all of your heart!

One's expression of passion is unique to each person and completely contingent upon one's personality. Some people will express their passionate tell God to "Leave!" pleading through tears. Others may plead their case through escalating the tone of their voice. Still others will exhibit their passions by preparing a well-framed series of thoughts that telegraph to the listener a high level of respect for their time. But however your pleading is expressed, remember to include the other two principles from 2 Timothy 4:2 about how to share God's truth.

Passionate pleading must involve precision and patience.

PRECISION

Notice that as soon as the Bible instructs the Christian to passionately "preach," it then pinpoints what should be said and how the proclaimer should say it. We need to be precise (accurate) when we share the truths of God's Word.

"Preach the Word; be prepared in season and out of season; correct, rebuke and encourage – with great patience and careful instruction."
(2 Timothy 4:2)

Preach "the Word." This term refers to the full council of God's truth. Ultimately, this "full council" of God's truth was collected within the covers of the Holy Bible (Old and New Testaments). But at the time of the writing of this statement, all of the biblical writings had not yet been written. Therefore, the Bible encourages the proclaimer to hold fast to God's view of the world and His relationship to it rather than to mankind's logic.

God's worldview is in stark contrast to mankind's natural logic, which is imperfect, sinful, and tarnished. Man's logic is incapable of giving ultimate clarity to things that pertain to living a godly life. In contrast, God is perfect—all-powerful, all-knowing, and all-present. "His divine power has given us everything we need for life and godliness through our knowledge of him who called us by his own glory and goodness" (2 Peter 1:3).That is why the Bible encourages us to stick to God's message of truth provided within its pages.

In preaching the full council of God's truth, we are sometimes called upon to "correct, rebuke and encourage" others in the faith. Correcting and rebuking are difficult assignments, both for the deliverer and the receiver. But it must be done prayerfully and in humility with love. None of us are above reproach, so if the Body of Christ is healthy and functioning according to biblical principles, at some point in our lives we will be on both the giving and receiving ends of being corrected, rebuked and encouraged. The Apostle Paul encouraged this same idea in First Thessalonians. "And we urge you brothers, warn those who are idle, encourage the timid, help the weak, be patient with everyone." (1 Thessalonians 5:14)

After establishing what should be proclaimed, the majority of this biblical statement instructs us on how we ought to passionately deliver such a message. Notice the two words at the end of 2 Timothy 4:2, "careful instruction." They refer to a thoughtful, careful presentation of and a precise pleading of God's Truth.

The Bible is reolete with reminders to make sure that every proclaimer remains precise in his/her pleading to another. Take for example what the Apostle Peter wrote to us in this regard. "But in your hearts set apart Christ as Lord. Always be prepared to give an answer to everyone who asks you to give the reason for the hope that you have. But do this with gentleness and respect" (1 Peter 3:15). The Greek word translated "an answer" in this translation is actually the first century word that denotes the type of answer that a lawyer provides in a courtroom—a well-prepared, seasoned, balanced, wise response.

Try to imagine how a lawyer prepares for a court case. He takes every person and detail into account in order to dictate how to present the case in court. It is done in a thoughtful fashion. He has to take into account the emotions of the family members, both for the plaintiff and defendant, who are emotionally stirred for opposite reasons. He has to take into account the media outlets that are recording and spinning every word. He remains mindful of the plaintiff's lawyer who is listening with a keen ear and parsing every predicate in order to attack at every point. He tactfully pleads to the senses of a diverse jury whose week has been disrupted by this summons to serve. All the while, the lawyer has to stay within the framework of the legal procedures that are refereed by an experienced judge. The lawyer must keep all of these details in mind as he presents his case to be judged by the people.

Can he lose his temper? No way. Can he present a weak case? Not if he doesn't want to lose. He needs to have his words chosen wisely and his eye on the end goal of earning a successful hearing with the people so they will come to agree with his point of view. This is exactly the stance we need to adopt as we discuss spiritual truth with others if we are going to ask them to sincerely consider adopting them into their heart and lives.

PATIENCE

The third point from 2 Timothy 4:2 furthers the "how" component of the Apostle Paul's instructions about the way we ought to ask people to consider spiritual truth. Patience is one of those attributes that few of us have developed. And the more technological society becomes, we have fewer opportunities to practice the art of patience. We have instant, simultaneous communication all around the world. For most of us, waiting isn't an option—we want "whatever" NOW! So how does our impatient culture handle the instruction in 2 Timothy 4:2?

"Preach the Word; be prepared in season and out of season; correct, rebuke and encourage – with great patience and careful instruction."

We have noticed that when encounters with those of different faiths "stall out," it's not necessarily because the points and counterpoints presented by Christians are faulty. It's been our observation that it's the method, not the message that drives away the unbelieving listener. Many Christians believe that the entire presentation of the gospel's truth (including the conversion of the listener) must always take place in the very first conversation ever held between the two parties. But that is not what occurred in many encounters that Jesus had during His earthly ministry.

Granted, sometimes the seed has been planted and watered, and you get to reap the harvest on your first encounter with someone, but that is not the norm. We humans don't typically trust a stranger, so why would we expect anyone to trust what we say upon meeting for the first time? Jesus understood this principle. He demonstrated patience in His encounter with that man who was a social outcast in the Mark 5 story. When the people asked Him to leave, Jesus respected their request and He quietly left. He didn't argue with them or give them a list of verses to memorize. He didn't even pray with them. Jesus realized that more often than not, there is a process that involves steps of further investigation and understanding before one adopts the truth of the gospel. He respected their request and trusted His Heavenly Father with the timing of their salvation.

A BALANCING ACT

Talking to people about spiritual truths is indeed a balancing act. We need to be both passionate yet patient. We need to be precise but also to listen precisely to the comments and concerns that the listener is trying to express so as to most appropriately respond. And we certainly must remember that truth can profoundly impact a heart, so we must sometimes allow them to process all the implications that truth will require of them.

It takes balance. Have you ever been presented facts or details about a situation and then asked immediately for your opinion on the issue at hand? We have. And what we noticed most about ourselves is that we are not quick to give an answer right away. We too find ourselves preferring to patiently process the information in a thoughtful manner.

Talking to people about spiritual truths is indeed a balancing act because you feel a certain level of urgency in one sense, yet you need to remain patient and wait on God's timing. The people who passionately share the truth of Jesus Christ are often rejected— not because of the truth of the message, but rather for the unbridled lack of control in their presentation. In their zeal they reach a level of force in either their tone of voice or in their personal demeanor that detracts the listener's attention away from the message and redirects the listener's full attention to reacting to the messenger's forceful tone and/or demeanor.

It's true. Passion is necessary for showing someone that you really believe what you are saying. But if you lose sight of the role of passion in your presentation, and you ignore the position and emotions of the listener, it can be so offensive the listener ultimately will miss the message.

It's also true that Jesus spoke as "one who had authority" (Matthew 7:29), but this did not mean He spoke abrasively or rudely. Actually, this verse refers to the fact that Jesus spoke as if He had the authority to speak on the issues because He Himself was the source of truth (i.e. "not as their teachers of the law" who referenced each other to gain an authoritative status). Thus, even though there were a few times Jesus addressed people with the equal force that they were attacking Him, generally, if the people were not hostile to Him, Jesus was not unnecessarily forceful in return.

It's all about demonstrating patience while maintaining a level of urgency. We are eager to share the truth because we sense a level of urgency for those outside the family of God. Yet, we must remember that we are merely the messengers. Our role is to deliver the truth with passionate pleading and precise accuracy. Then we must be patient and trust the Lord with the timing of bringing understanding into their hearts.

THE GOAL

We recommend that you adopt Paul's balanced approach as recorded in Acts 17:2-3. We know that after his conversion, Paul's zeal landed him in several jails! But these verses indicate that somewhere along the way, Paul learned how to balance his passion with patience when he was presenting the truth.

Acts 17:2-3 confirms that he exhibited a patient, calm, and controlled resoluteness when he spoke to others. "As was his custom, Paul went into the synagogue, and on three Sabbath days he reasoned with them from the Scriptures, explaining and proving that the Messiah had to suffer and rise from the dead."

Later on in Acts 17, Paul shares a few verses about the varied responses he got from people. We shouldn't be surprised at the diverse reactions we will receive when spiritual truths are presented. "And when they heard of the resurrection of the dead, some mocked, while others said, 'We will hear you again on this matter.' So Paul departed from among them. However, some men joined him and believed, among them Dionysius the Areopagite, a woman named Damaris, and others with them" (Acts 17:32-34).

True impact can only happen when people are not coaxed or tricked into believing what we believe is the truth. Life change happens when they embrace their need for a Savior. At the point in time when they understand that Jesus Christ is the sinless Son of God who came to earth, who died and rose again, and who is the only One able to pay for their sins, then they have a choice to make. We can continue to pray for them, but we must remember that it is their choice, and the timing is out of our hands.

LET US REASON

Now that we have introduced some of the emotional impacts of having spiritual conversations with people, in the pages to follow, we will talk in length about the cognitive impact to considering spiritual truth. Meaning, if we are going to ask people to "consider" spiritual truth and "reason" with us about it, then it goes without saying that we need to be logical thinkers that are able to soundly reason with people. Thus, we are going to discuss how to become a critical thinker, what a "worldview" is, and whether or not it is logical to adopt some worldviews that are proposed today.

In the coming days, you may feel like a member of that crowd on the beach whose eyes were opened to the truth about Jesus Christ, and you may come to submit your heart and life to Him. Or, you may feel a bit fearful because you may take what you learn about becoming a critical thinker and begin to see that your current belief system is not holding up in the face of sound scrutiny. Still, you may feel a bit desensitized about what you read because you have at some point in your life decided that you never had to place your own beliefs under the microscope to see if they stand critical scrutiny. And, for some reason, others may feel initially hostile at the thought of being asked to consider the things that will be addressed in the subsequent pages. And for whatever reason, this segment of readers will lash out at anyone who enters into discussion with them about these issues of life.

USE THIS TIME WISELY

Wherever you are in your spiritual life, we encourage you to make the most out of this opportunity as you focus your mind on these spiritual issues in the coming days. We would ask that you take the journey. Talk about it with friends, classmates, professors, colleagues, pastors, and fellow parishioners. Devote this time to ask the questions you may have never had the courage to ask before. Use this time to reflect on the decisions that you have placed the eternity of your soul upon and come up with a clear, definite answer and conclusion to what you believe about God and your relationship to Him. And determine that by the end of your time with us, you will have certainty about how to have peace in your soul for all eternity.

Take full advantage of this time!

CHAPTER **TWO**

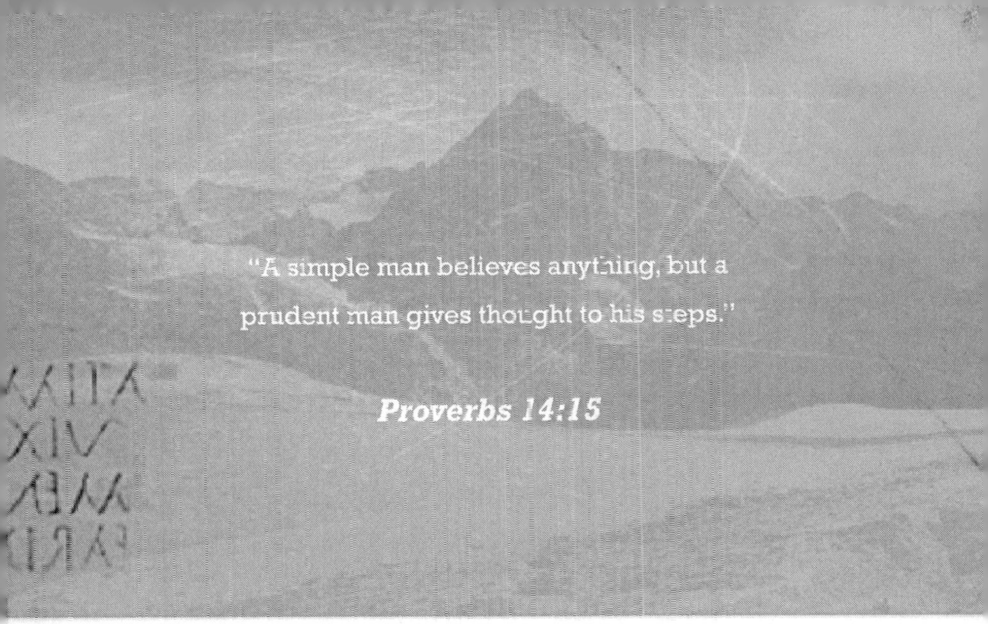

"A simple man believes anything, but a prudent man gives thought to his steps."

Proverbs 14:15

CRITICAL THINKING

WHAT WAS HE THINKING?!

How many times have we said these words out loud as we watch reality home videos on television? You know the kind—the people who will do anything to get on TV! Like the guy that took his sled up onto the roof after a heavy snowfall. His bravado was showing all over as he stood on the roof, waving his sled for all to see. The stunt he intended to perform was to go sledding off of his roof and happily land on the deck below. No doubt he thought that all of that snow would help him make the perfect soft landing. Boy was he wrong! It was a brutal scene. He made a crash landing onto the deck. There was no more bravado. His body was crumpled in a heap in the midst of the splintered pieces of his sled. What was he thinking?

His passion to attempt the impossible overshadowed his ability to think at all. We often have to set aside our passion in order to think clearly, to think critically, in order to make wise decisions.

CRITICAL THINKING

It is a common practice we do every day, but we may never even be aware of it. For example, in the English language, how do you know whether the word "r-e-a-d" should be understood as a directive to "read a book," or if it is to be understood as a past-tense word describing a moment that someone "had already read that book last week?"

Critical thinking.

Another example is with the word "conflict." Do we have a "conflict" (i.e. a moment of tense disagreement) occurring between our children? Or, does our view "conflict" with another's view (i.e. to be contradictory, used as a verb)? How do we know the difference?

Critical thinking.

What is the difference between "supervision" and "oversight?" Break those two words apart (super-vision and over-sight) and you have "super" correlating with the word "over," and you have "vision" looking pretty similar to the word "sight." But I think you would agree that there is a difference between someone who has 'supervision' over an entire department and when that same employee forgets to perform an important task and apologizes for his 'oversight.'

Critical thinking.

In each of the examples above, understanding the context is necessary in the process of critical thinking. Discernment is needed in every area of our lives, but the path to discernment is through critical thinking. Some in American culture even reject the idea of questioning what another person believes by championing the idea of tolerance and pluralism. What a person believes is important and being able to critically think and to intelligently challenge incorrect thinking is essential in the process of making wise decisions in life.

WHAT IS CRITICAL THINKING?

Critical thinking is a self-guided, self-disciplined process which directs individuals to think correctly about themselves and the world around them. It is an essential method that guides its adherents toward truth. It involves investigation, analysis and self-corrective decision-making which provide a consistent and coherent way to solve problems and come to conclusions. 4

The word critical comes from the Greek word kritikos from which the English word "critic" is derived. It means to judge or to discern, to make sense of, to recognize and comprehend. It is through the process of questioning what is read, heard, seen and experienced that you can come to the best possible conclusion about a matter in order to make wise decisions.

Unfortunately, some who go through the process of critical thinking become disillusioned and skeptical of everything. That is not the intention of this chapter or this book. Instead, we want to challenge you to "know what you believe" and "why you believe it." "For the word of God is living and active. Sharper than any double-edged sword, it penetrates even to dividing soul and spirit, joints and marrow; it judges the thoughts and attitudes of the heart" (Hebrews 4:12).

Humans have the unique ability to think and to make discriminating choices. Homo sapiens means "thinking man." As supported in Scripture, the image of God refers to the fact that we human beings have the same intellect, emotion, and will as God has . . . but not to the extent of God's infinite omniscient (all-knowingness), perfect understanding. God's emotions are derived from His divine holiness.

However, not all humans "think" well. For example, it doesn't take too long for a professor in a classroom to notice the obvious stirring of emotions of students when asked to contemplate something that is foreign to what they have been told all their lives, but they have never considered its rationale. We experience this regularly when we present the truth of forgiveness from God through Jesus Christ . . .shudder, squirm, sigh. They have never been challenged to evaluate their own beliefs. They have just adopted the beliefs of others. Therefore, if you want to be a balanced "critical" thinker, it is imperative that you follow these three important steps:

1. ***Rehearse:*** You must evaluate the evidence and "so-called" opinions.
2. ***Reflect:*** You must reflect on the meaning of statements and ideas.
3. ***Reason:*** You must test the reasonableness of statements and ideas.

Rehearse: Recognize and evaluate the evidence and "so-called" opinions.

When people provide their position on a particular issue, we say that they offer their opinion. For example, some people prefer deep, dark, warm, rich colors and others prefer florescent colors like hot pink, lime green and bright turquoise. Some of us love the beach and others of us love the mountains. These opinions about our personal preferences are neither right nor wrong—they are based on how we are wired. But when it comes to our opinions about a specific topic or an issue, it gets a little more complicated. Everyone has a right to share their opinion about a particular issue, but all opinions must be scrutinized to determine how much credence one should give to that particular opinion. In other words, everyone has a right to an opinion, but that does not make every opinion accurate and correct. And because it is a personal thought, it has the propensity to be consistent or inconsistent, logical or illogical, factual or non-factual. While it is true that opinions are formulated throughout one's life experience – and experiences are indeed valuable – it does not guarantee that a person's opinion will therefore be normative, or what every other person should adhere to. For people who have no desire to persuade another to adopt their opinion on an issue, they are simply sharing their "preference." But a person who wishes for his/her opinion to be adopted by another, their view must be formulated based upon sound evidence, and not just emotions and/or individual perspectives.

As a critical thinker you must be able to recognize if the opinion is based upon sound evidence or based upon personal preference. And the only way in which someone is able to process evidence critically is to do his/her own proper and sound investigation and evaluation of the information presented to determine if it was accurately obtained and factual.

Therefore, each person who desires to think critically must be committed to asking the "Who/What/Where/When/Why/How" questions. It is necessary to ask these questions prior to declaring something as sound and reliable evidence upon which to hold a sound opinion.

Reflect: Reflect on the meaning and significance of statements and ideas.

A critical thinker must be intentional about reflection. Reflection in this context refers to the process by which you contemplate the meaning of the statement, the motive of the statement, and the level of significant impact of the statement.

When you hear a statement or an idea, it can have enormous implications. You should ask yourself, "What did they mean by that?" "Is that significant to my life?" So often people hear, but they do not listen. Statements and ideas are presented, and they are assumed to be true or false. Many times they are misunderstood or even worse, ignored

The practice of reflection is often a momentary experience that occurs throughout the day. Or some have found it beneficial to take a day or a week-end to reflect on personal and professional goals. However, most of your reflection time will only take a few moments, but its value should not be negated. Reflection can help you at home with personal decisions, at your job with business obligations, and in spiritual matters of the heart. It should become an important part of your daily life which allows you to process information correctly instead of in a reactionary way. How many times have you seen someone react to what they heard only to find out his or her perceptions were inaccurate? Reflection is necessary for a proper response.

Reason: Test the reasonableness of statements and ideas.

Have you ever heard the phrase, "If it sounds too good to be true, it probably is!"? Critical thinking is the process of evaluating the reasonableness of statements and ideas before acting upon them or passing them along as truth. Unfortunately, many people have been duped by internet scams, fraudulent mail and phone calls as well as many other ways simply because they didn't think it through before responding. Regrettably, many people assume that if it is in print, or someone of reputation reportedly said it, then it must be true. False! All you have to do is look up some of the most notable websites that are established to debunk the many false statements and ideas that are being sent across the internet and other mediums. We must hone our critical thinking skills and be aware of the many scams that are around every corner.

Now, let's touch on a really sensitive subject for many Christians. What about preachers? The authors of this book are both ministers. Every week we are in front of hundreds of people. So, how do we feel confident that what we are saying should be adopted and adhered to?

We firmly believe that Christians should not be exempt from critical analysis. When we present the truths of the Bible, we welcome our audience to critically rehearse, reflect, and reason regarding what has been presented about the Christian faith. In our lives we have seen many critical thinkers contemplate the teachings of the Bible only to become persuaded as to the sound evidence and logic of the Christian faith. Fortunately, in addition to the number of evidences for the Christian faith found within the Bible, its validity is also reinforced by testimonies of how these evidences altered the lives of some key people in history.

The Apostle Paul, the writer of the majority of the New Testament, is considered to be the greatest apologist of Christianity, and he was tested. In the book of Acts, the author, Luke, illustrated this process of critical thinking when he stated, "Now the Bereans were of more noble character than the Thessalonians, for they received the message with great eagerness and examined the Scriptures every day to see if what Paul said was true" (Acts 17:11).

Give Yourself an Honest Look.

To become a critical thinker you should develop some positive daily activities that will become habits over time. These habits can be challenging to incorporate into your life, especially if you've already established a habit which is contrary to critical thinking. However, like any bad habit, it can be overcome by practicing the right action long enough.

Constantly evaluate your own beliefs, attitudes, values and opinions. Why do you believe what you believe? Is your attitude correct? What do you value and why is it important to you? How have you formulated your opinions— and are they true? These are the types of questions that critical thinkers ask of themselves and others. These questions are important because your answers can influence your beliefs which will ultimately affect your behavior.

For example, some people believe God loves them because it was something they were told since childhood. As long as their life is happy and free from conflict this belief goes unchallenged. Then, something tragic happens. A family member becomes ill and is expected to die. They still believe God loves them. They expect Him to answer their prayers and heal their family member. But their belief in a loving God is challenged when the family member passes away. What their belief is based upon will greatly impact whether or not they continue to believe that God loves them. It will determine whether they run into His arms for comfort, or run away from Him in anger and bitterness.

Make time to take an honest look at your own beliefs, attitudes, values and opinions. These characteristics are the heart of who you are. It's challenging to look into the mirror, but it is absolutely necessary not only to evaluate, but also to develop your own beliefs, attitudes, values and opinions based on biblical principles.

- ***Do not pretend to know what you do not know.***

People are sometimes asked questions that they don't know the answer to, but they act as if they are an expert in the subject. Listening to their response can be very frustrating. Sometimes they use technical words, trying to impress the listeners, but the audience is often left disillusioned.

Let's face it, it is impossible to know everything. The more you read and investigate information, the more you come to an understanding of how little you actually know. Don't get discouraged. Gaining knowledge is a lifelong process. As the Apostle Paul encouraged the church at Ephesus, "Let us not become weary in doing good, for at the proper time we will reap a harvest if we do not give up" (Galatians 6:9).

What is the best way to handle a situation when you are asked a question in which you don't know the answer? Admit that you don't know it. You might respond like this: "That's a great question but I don't know the answer to it." However, don't leave the question unanswered indefinitely. Either agree to get the answer to them later, or better yet, investigate the answer together, if possible.

Do not blindly adhere to tradition.

Traditions can be a very important part of your personal and family life. Some of these traditions are passed from generation to generation and others may have just been started. Traditions can be personal values that we would like to pass on to others or important customs that are shared during family mealtimes, or on special holidays, birthdays, and vacations. Important religious beliefs, events and activities can also be traditions which are passed on to our children and grandchildren. Because of the nature of religious traditions, they can be perceived as necessary to be accepted by future generations. They can be very personal as well as very volatile.

Although traditions are very important, critical thinkers should not blindly follow those traditions unless they embody God's truth. However, sometimes children follow the religious traditions of their family because they are afraid of offending someone. But what if following that tradition impacts your eternity? What if you are so concerned about offending a family member that you reject God? For example, what if you remain faithful to a religious group your whole life even though you question or know that what is being taught is not true. Rather than breaking from tradition you pacify your family but deny the truth. Is it really worth risking an eternity in Heaven?

Seek clarification of terms.

Have you ever read a book, newspaper or magazine and you came across an unfamiliar word? What did you do? Did you just keep reading or did you take the time to look it up in an online dictionary? Honestly, most people just keep reading in hopes that it will all make sense in the context. However, that is not always the case. The definitions of words are very important.

I (Lew) remember taking a drive with my father and two young daughters. We drove through our local park and my dad wanted to share with my girls the story of how he proposed to my mom at this same park. As we drove around a bend next to a small pond my father said, "Hey girls, that's where your grandmother and I made love." I instantly looked into the back seat and I could tell by their faces it was more than they wanted to know. However, growing up hearing this story I knew what he meant, so I asked him to clarify. He said, "Oh, that's where the park ranger caught your grandmother and me kissing after I proposed to her. It was past curfew so he asked us to leave." What a sigh of relief came from the back seat!

Terms can impact your perception of truth. For example, what did Paul and Silas mean when they said to the keeper of the prison, "Believe in the Lord Jesus, and you will be saved." (Acts 16:31). Did they mean that he only needed to believe in the historical Jesus? Did they mean that he needed to believe that Jesus was Lord? If you know the original language you can come to an understanding much easier. But what if you don't know Greek? Then you must rely on other methods to come to know the truth. You can see how the word is used in other passages in the Bible, or you can use a good Bible commentary. The solution is that you understand what it means so that you can also be confident when you share it with others.

Explore the many sides of an issue.

Are you a person who likes to live in your comfort zone? What happens to you when change occurs? Do you embrace it or avoid it? Most of us don't like change because of how it can impact our daily lives. Learning new information and changing your mind about something can make you feel uncomfortable. However, that should not deter the critical thinker.

Have you ever been asked to give a persuasive speech or write a paper on a particular topic in which you have a strong opinion? How did you go about researching your topic? Did you investigate the various sides or opinions on the topic? Unfortunately, when many students research a subject for a speech or a writing assignment they begin with a presupposition they assume to be true. They have a belief about the truthfulness of a matter and they begin to do their research, seeking arguments and evidence to support their belief while they ignore arguments and evidence to the contrary. This approach in logic has a technical name that will be discussed in more detail in Chapter 3.

Critical thinkers should attempt to find and avoid bias in their own arguments as well as in the arguments of others. When researching a topic it is important to investigate the many sides of an issue and come to a conclusion based upon the best information available. But what if you find that the information you learn is the opposite of what you believe to be true? Two things should happen at that point. First, you must evaluate if you have obtained the most accurate information, covering all sides of the subject to validate your research. You may come to a wrong conclusion because the information you obtained was biased or skewed. If you find that to be the case, you may need to continue your research. The second option you have is to change your opinion. It is always appropriate to admit, "I was wrong." Some of these changes in belief can have little ultimate significance. But other changes in belief can have major consequences, including those that involve eternity.

Be eager to learn from your own experiences as well as the experiences of others.

I (Lew) remember the day my father and mother dropped me off at college for the first time. I was filled with all kinds of emotions, and I will never forget the advice my father gave me just before pulling away. He told me to gain as many new experiences as possible because it would broaden me as a person. What he was trying to teach me was a principle of critical thinking.

Experience can be a great teacher. Throughout your life you will have the opportunity to experience new things. Some experiences are good and some of them are bad, but both can be your teachers to help you live a more educated and productive life. That is why experience is an important component in gaining employment. This is not to minimize the value of an education, but experience provides you with the knowledge to ask good questions and to know the right questions to ask. Experience provides the catalyst to enhance your education

If you wanted to learn about Christian missions how would you go about it? Well, you could go to a Christian bookstore and purchase a book on missions. You could also take a course in missions and hopefully your professor was formerly a missionary so you could gain his or her first-hand experience. You could also go hear a missionary speak at your local church or attend a missions conference. All of these are good things which will help you to learn about missions. Probably the best way to learn about missions is actually to visit the mission field with an experienced missionary. This way you can experience it for yourself and gain personal knowledge that will impact your thinking. It can also eliminate false ideas or inaccurate perceptions of what the mission field and missionaries are really like. This is true regarding most topics. Experience does have its limitations. However, critical thinkers are eager to learn from their own experiences as well as the experiences of others so that they will have a better opportunity to make informed decisions.

LOOKING AHEAD

We want you to be "thinking" men and women, so you make wise decisions throughout your life's journey. This chapter was a good primer to encourage you to be a critical thinker. We focused on how important it is to evaluate a statement to determine if those words are based on sound evidence, or if the statement is merely someone's personal preference. Critical thinkers look at all the sides of an issue, and they ask the "Who/What/Where/When/Why/How" questions before they determine their position. The next chapter is a look at how people often present faulty reasoning in their quest to change another person's beliefs. It's important for critical thinkers to recognize these fallacies because that recognition could be the catalyst to help someone discover the truth.

CHAPTER **THREE**

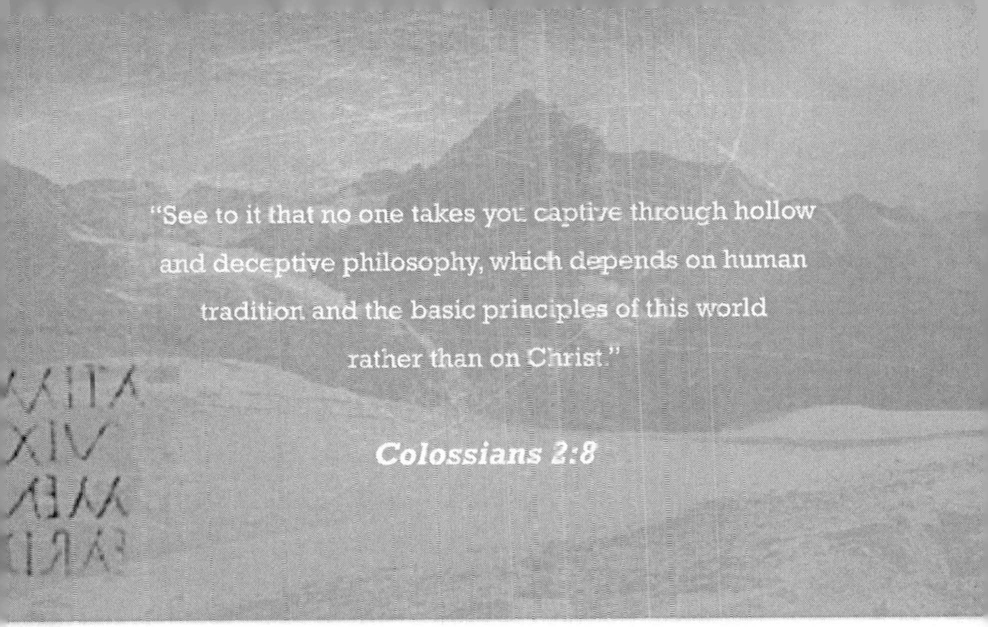

RIGHT QUESTIONS GET RIGHT ANSWERS

ASKING THE RIGHT QUESTIONS

When you were a child and your parents asked you to do something, did you ever ask , "Why?" And did you ever hear the response, "Because I said so."? If you are a parent, have you ever said that to your child(ren)? How did it go? What reason did you have for responding that way? Was it legitimate or did you honestly just not have the energy to explain yourself? Was it the right way to respond?

Questions and answers like these between parents and children are often very common and at times appropriate. Parents rightly see themselves in an authoritative role in which they expect compliance or agreement. A problem with critical thinking can exist, though, when children grow up not knowing how or why to ask the right questions. This will directly affect their ability to make good decisions.

All of us are bombarded with information from all types of sources. Which ones can be trusted? Who should be believed and why? Every day we are faced with new ideas, beliefs and opinions that need our response. Some of our choices have minimal consequences such as when we choose to buy an advertised product. Sometimes we are glad we purchased it, and other times we realize the claims made in the advertisement were just not true. Other decisions we make can have more lasting consequences like choosing a major at college, accepting an offer for employment, or deciding on the right person to marry. There are three primary approaches all of us take when making decisions:

1. Indecision
2. Passive Decision-Making
3. Active Decision-Making

Indecision

Indecision—not making a decision—is actually a decision in itself. There are times when indecision is necessary because you do not have all of the facts needed to make an informed choice. In these cases it is prudent to reserve judgment for a later time. However, never coming to a conclusion about a matter can be unwise and at times foolish. Imagine you have been given the responsibility to defuse a bomb before it explodes. You carefully open the panel, exposing the wires. You know you have to cut one of the wires, but which one? Is it the green wire or the red wire? You can choose not to decide, but eventually the bomb will explode and its impact can affect you and/or others.

Do you know individuals who have come to the same conclusion regarding spiritual matters? They have heard the truth about God and Jesus, but they just put off making a decision. They think they will have time in the future to make a choice. But for many, death comes before the choice is made and indecision becomes the decision.

Passive Decision-Making

The second approach is passive decision-making. This approach is taken when a person chooses not to evaluate what they see or hear. They just accept the opinions of others as truth, thus making someone else's opinion their own without ever applying critical thinking skills. Using the bomb analogy, it would be like choosing a wire based upon the opinion of an inquisitive person standing next to you. You ask them, "Which wire should I cut?" They say, "Cut the red one" and you cut it. Two things might occur at this point. The bomb might be defused and everyone would be safe, or the bomb could explode and you and others would die. Sometimes you get lucky by choosing the passive decision-making approach. But do you really want to live your life based on luck? We hope not.

Sometimes people approach spiritual decision-making in this passive way. They are brought up in a religious tradition, and they accept it as truth because that's what they were told. Unfortunately, they never really investigated the truthfulness of their religious belief system, and they blindly accepted the traditions as truth. Should our future for all eternity be viewed as a matter of luck? Should people blindly accept their religious beliefs and traditions without investigation?

Active Decision-Making

The third approach is active decision-making. Everyone has to make important and/or difficult choices. When that happens to you, what process do you go through to make the best decision? Active decision-making is a process of asking the right questions of yourself and others to come to the best possible conclusion. These questions might include:

What is the decision I must make?

What values do I need to incorporate in making this decision?

What do I need to know in order to make a wise decision?

Can I trust the sources I am using to make this decision?

What alternatives are available within the scope of this decision?

Have I investigated the issue enough to make an informed decision?

Am I willing to make a decision and follow through on my decision?

Again, if we use the bomb illustration, how would an active decision maker decide which wire to cut? Let's use the questions above to illustrate the third approach. First, I must defuse this bomb. I need to do this because lives are at stake and human life is precious. I need to know which wire to cut. What does the person next to me really know about defusing a bomb? Nothing! Ok, I am not going to take his or her opinion. Is there anyone else around who knows how to defuse a bomb, or is there an instruction guide to use? Someone just handed me a phone with a person who defused bombs in the military, and he knows how to defuse this bomb. I have the right information to help me. If I don't defuse this bomb the only alternative is that it will probably explode. I have the best person possible to help me make this decision so I shouldn't delay any longer. I have got to cut one of these wires. Based upon the best information possible, I am cutting the green wire. The bomb is defused.

Spiritually, an active decision-maker understands that a decision needs to be made about their religious belief system. They need to know the biblical truth, and they need to be willing to investigate the truthfulness of God's Word as well as their current belief system. Once they have investigated it to the best of their ability, they will come to a decision and by faith act upon that decision.

As we present biblical truth to those seeking answers, it is our responsibility to communicate that the gospel message is not based on a blind leap of faith, but rather it is based on sound reasoning and historical evidence. It is important to clarify that the terms biblical truth, spiritual truth, gospel, gospel message, and salvation all refer to the basic tenets on which believing Christians base their faith.

WHAT IS AN ARGUMENT?

Have you ever had an argument with someone? What is the first thing you assume when you argue with someone? Did you answer, "I'm right."? What is the second thing you assume? "They're wrong" is the common response. It is interesting to note that at the core of these assumptions is the idea that there is an ultimate right and wrong with regards to opinions.

When you think of the word argument, what comes to your mind? Do you envision a heated exchange between two or more people? That is a common interpretation. However, that is not the approach of this book. We are defining this term in its classical philosophical sense rather than how we commonly understand and use it.

An argument is an attempt to offer evidence to demonstrate the soundness of an opinion. An opinion is a personal belief or a conclusion about an issue or a topic. It can be the result of using critical thinking or simply an emotional response to information presented. Opinions are often changed when the argument presented is more reasonable than competing arguments because it is supported by better evidence and/or reasons. Arguments can be sound (logical) or unsound (illogical). Coming to a conclusion about a matter involves investigating the evidence or reasons for a belief to determine if it is sound and believable.

What is the purpose of an argument? It is intended to change another person's beliefs. Depending upon how you argue will determine if you are actually changing another person's mind or making an enemy. It will determine if you have helped someone discover the truth or if you have manipulated them into giving lip service to your beliefs, but they do not really accept them as fact.

WHAT IS EVIDENCE?

Evidence is the basis or cause of a belief. It is a statement of justification and explanation of a belief or an action. It answers the questions, "Why do you believe...?" or "Why did you do that?" There are two primary ways evidence is gathered: personal experience and data gained from an external source.

The evidence of personal experience is one way data is obtained to develop an argument. The Apostle Paul used this approach when he was given permission by King Agrippa to defend himself at his trial in Acts 26. As a part of his argument Paul shares his personal experience of being confronted by the risen Christ on the road to Damascus. At the end of Paul's argumentation, after hearing the evidence, King Agrippa said to Festus and Bernice, "This man is not doing anything that deserves death or imprisonment"(Acts 26:31). Paul had won his argument with King Agrippa. Personal experiences can be very effective and persuasive to people who find personal experience more appealing than a list of facts and empirical data. However, personal experience is limited in its ability to be persuasive since it cannot necessarily be proven to be true and should not be relied upon completely in the development of an argument.

Evidence can also be gathered through external sources. Examples of external evidence include the eyewitness testimony of others, expert opinions, statistical reports and analysis, published reports in magazines, journals or even newspapers, etc. In 1 Corinthians 15, Paul uses the eyewitness testimony of others as he presents an apologetic for Christianity to the church at Corinth. He begins his argument by stating "For what I received I passed on to you as of first importance: that Christ died for our sins according to the Scriptures" (1 Corinthians 15:3). He then proceeds to attempt to give evidence of the resurrection of Christ through the eyewitness testimonies of others. Paul had his own experience, but he also was told about the experiences of others which he was now using as evidence for his claim.

John the Baptist, while in prison, sent two of his disciples to ask Jesus, "Are you the one who was to come, or should we expect someone else" (Matthew 11:3)? Jesus then proceeds to provide evidence of being the Son of God and the Coming Messiah by telling the disciples to tell John, "The blind receive sight, the lame walk, those who have leprosy are cured, the deaf hear, the dead are raised, and the good news is preached to the poor" (Matthew 11:5). Again, Paul not only uses eyewitness testimony but also the evidence of events that defy natural laws and they didn't happen in a controlled environment. People saw Jesus heal the sick and raise the dead, not on a stage but in the arena of everyday life.

Evidence must also be evaluated before it is presented as fact. A critical thinker should investigate the quality of the support to determine if the evidence is legitimate. Expert opinion can be used as evidence to support a claim. However, as we all know, experts disagree with each other about the same issue even when using the same data. It can take multiple types of evidence to come to a sound conclusion.

FALLACIES USED IN ARGUMENTS

There are numerous fallacies used in presenting arguments. A fallacy is simply any error, whether intentional or unintentional, in reasoning. The most common kinds of fallacies are informal in nature. Think of them as counterfeit arguments. The following is presented as a sampling of informal logical fallacies (listed alphabetically). It is not intended to be an exhaustive treatise on the subject, but rather a collection of notable fallacies along with their basic definition and a few examples to help you understand them in a practical way. Although you may not always remember their names, the most important thing is to be able to recognize them in your argumentation and in the arguments of others.

AD HOMINEM FALLACY

Ad Hominem literally means "To the Man." This fallacy seeks to discredit a person's argument by attacking their personal character, origin, associations, etc., rather than their ideas. It is often used when one person realizes that he cannot defend his beliefs, so he attempts to win an argument in a popular way through personal or humorous attacks.

Example #1 – A politician will attack the opponent personally rather than attack the opponent's ideas to win a campaign. It becomes a popularity contest rather than being focused to choose the best qualified candidate who represents the people's values. In a debate a question is raised regarding abstinence education and one of the candidates says, "Here is my opponent, speaking to you of the values of abstinence and abstinence education when everyone knows she had a child out of wedlock while she was a teenager herself!" The argument says nothing about the issue of abstinence education, but it concentrates on the fact that the other candidate had a child as a teenager before she was married.

Example #2 – A person discredits another person's argument by calling them a name or by describing a derogatory attribute. "Sue can't be right because she's a moron." Calling Sue a name doesn't address the truthfulness of her argument at all. It is just a method used by some to disregard her arguments.

APPEAL TO AUTHORITY FALLACY

The Appeal to Authority argument is used when a person appeals to the opinions of an expert in a field rather than doing their own research. It is assumed that their conclusions are true based solely on their reputation. It is also used when a person appeals to the authority of a popular, well-liked person, who is respected by the audience, but the person has no real authority on the matter.

Example #1 – Dan Barker, in his book Godless, argues against the idea that the universe we live in is not unique, but there are many potential universes like our own. He states, "Many or most cosmologists are now convinced that some kind of multiverse is likely. A multiverse is a collection of universes, and there are many scenarios." The assumption is made that these cosmologists are correct without investigating their research. (Citation: Dan Barker. Godless. Ulysses Press 2008, p. 109.)

Example #2 – Many advertisers use celebrities to market their products because they are well respected. It doesn't mean that they are an expert in the product they are advertising. They are being paid to catch the attention of the audience and sell the merchandise—period. The advertising company is using the Appeal to Authority argument in hopes of convincing you to buy their product.

APPEAL TO IGNORANCE FALLACY

Appeal to Ignorance is used when a person claims something is true simply because it cannot be disproved, or that something is fictitious because it cannot be proven to be true.

Example #1 – The existence of God, either the affirmation or the negation of His existence is often argued using the Appeal to Ignorance. In the affirmative it is argued, "I know that God exists because no atheist, no matter how clever, has ever provided evidence to the contrary." It is also argued that God does not exist. "The only reality is what can be known through the senses, and since I cannot see God, He doesn't exist."

Example #2 – Conspiracy theories can be argued using this method as well. "The government is hiding the truth from us. I know that aliens exist because the government has not proven that they don't."

BANDWAGON FALLACY

The Bandwagon argument is used when a person justifies a course of action because "everyone else is doing it." This argument is often used when peer pressure (fear of rejection or promise of affection) causes a person to defend their action or inaction.

Example #1 –

Ellen: "Mom, can I get a tattoo?"

Mom: "No!"

Ellen: "That's not fair. Everyone at school is getting one for graduation."

Ellen is arguing on the basis of the fact that all of her friends are getting tattoos for graduation. However, she is offering no good evidence for her reason to get one.

Example #2 – "I cannot believe that the U.S., as civilized as it is, still allows the death penalty. Most other countries have already made capital punishment unlawful. How can the U.S. continue this barbaric practice? " In this example, the U.S. is accused of being immoral for allowing capital punishment. But what valid argument or arguments are given to indicate that capital punishment is immoral? None were given, so the argument is fallacious.

BEGGING THE QUESTION FALLACY

This argument is sometimes referred to as "circular reasoning." It occurs in an argument when a person assumes that their conclusion is true by the premise itself, or that the conclusion is supported by itself, or by simply restating the conclusion in a different way. Such an argument is Begging the Question, instead of answering it.

Example #1 – A Christian is asked to defend their belief that the Bible is true. Their response is to quote Scripture. "All Scripture is God-breathed and is useful for teaching, rebuking, correcting and training in righteousness" (2 Timothy 3:16). The argument then is that the Bible is true because the Bible says it's true. Unfortunately no evidence is given to support the conclusion other than the source itself. Can you see the circular reasoning? That would be like arguing that your opinion is right because it is your opinion. Other religious texts also claim to be true, but that argument alone does not make them true.

Example #2 – Capital punishment is the intentional killing of a human being and as such is murder. Murder is illegal. Thus, capital punishment should be illegal. Here again the conclusion is assumed in its premises. There is an assumption being made that capital punishment is equivalent to murder. Why is this assumed? What arguments are given to support that conclusion? There is none and that is why this argument is Begging the Question.

FALSE ANALOGY FALLACY

An analogy is a comparison of similarity between two things. A False Analogy occurs when an argument is formulated on the basis of a comparison of unrelated things. People often apply their knowledge of one thing and use it in conjunction with an unrelated area. Sometimes that approach is appropriate. For example, a preacher might use an example from nature to describe a spiritual truth. However, there are times when an argument is given but its comparison is not legitimate. A False Analogy has occurred.

Example #1 – A biology textbook instructs its readers about the evolution of arthropods. Examples of arthropods include the extinct trilobite, and modern day spiders, crabs, and butterflies. The argument in part is presented as follows: "The first arthropods occurred in the sea more than 600 million years ago. Since then, arthropods have moved into all parts of the sea, most freshwater habitats, the land, and the air . . . This early body plan was modified gradually. Body segments were lost or fused over time . . . Arthropod appendages also evolved into different forms that are adapted in ways that enable them to perform different functions. These appendages include antenna, claws, walking legs, wings, flippers, mouth parts, tails, and other specialized structures."

The authors then attempt to provide a practical example of this evolutionary process. "These gradual changes in arthropods are similar to the changes in modern cars since the Model T, the first mass-produced automobile. The Model T had all of the basic components, such as an internal combustion engine, wheels and a frame. Over time, the design changed, producing cars as different as off-road vehicles, sedans and sports cars. Similarly, modifications to the arthropod body plan have produced creatures as different as a tick and a lobster."

The False Analogy is evident by their comparison of a hypothetical evolutionary process change in arthropods with the intelligent design change of modern automobiles. Body parts from the Model T did not just fall off or fuse with other body parts to one day become a Lamborghini. (Citation: Miller, Kenneth R., Levine, Joseph, Biology, Prentice Hall, Upper Saddle River, NJ. 2004)

Example #2 – The term "Animal Auschwitz" can be found on many websites and in articles which are in opposition of the killing of animals for food. The analogy is made that the transporting and killing of animals for food is similar to the Nazi regime killing 6 million Jews in the Holocaust. We must be fair at this point. There are those who come from an Atheistic worldview belief system in which everything on this planet has evolved and humans are no more valuable than any living creature, so all life deserves to be protected whether animal or human. Animal Auschwitz is consistent with their worldview. However, some of these sites address animals as God's creation. In these cases they are coming from a theistic worldview which embraces the idea that man is unique and different from the animal kingdom. From a Judeo-Christian ethic, man is unique because of being created in God's image (Genesis 1:27). Thus the analogy of killing animals for food and the Nazi's killing 6 million Jews is not only a False Analogy but it's offensive. (Note: This is not an argument in favor of the mistreatment of animals. It is only addressing the False Analogy argument.)

FALSE DILEMMA OR EITHER/OR FALLACY

A False Dilemma occurs in an argument when a person oversimplifies a complex issue to make it appear that only two alternatives are possible. There are times when only two options exist. For example, there are only two choices in responding to the question, "Does God exist?" He either exists or He doesn't exist. There isn't a third alternative to choose from and the answer to that question doesn't commit this fallacy. However, when a False Dilemma does occur, you should ask yourself whether additional options are plausible.

Example #1 – "I am against children being home-schooled since I believe children need the social interaction that a traditional education provides. You must either send your child to a traditional school or you condemn your child into receiving an inferior education." For this to be true, you must assume that there are only two options possible. Is that the case? No. In today's world, there are multiple types of home-school education options that offer diverse learning and social programs.

Example #2 – "You are either for abortion or the only other option is for women to use backyard, unsterile abortion clinics where many will be injured and some will die." Although some women may choose to think that these unsterile clinics are their only option that clearly is not the case. Pro-life homes exist around the country to provide an alternative to abortion.

HASTY CONCLUSION FALLACY

A Hasty Conclusion occurs when one makes a judgment on the basis of one or even a few samples. This argument is used when a conclusion is made without enough evidence. When using critical thinking you want to have a good reason for why you have concluded something. In this case, it is necessary to continue to investigate before coming to a conclusion and especially before sharing that conclusion with someone else.

Example #1 – "My friend told me that her philosophy class was hard. I'm in a philosophy class and it's hard, too. All philosophy classes are hard." Although each person's experience may be real and true to them, the opinions of two individuals do not constitute enough evidence to prove the fact that all philosophy classes are hard.

Example #2 –

Ambrose: "James, have you tried out that new restaurant?"

James: "Yes, and it was awful. The service was terrible and the food didn't taste good at all. I am never going back."

(Later that day)

Maryann: "Ambrose, have you tried out that new restaurant?"

Ambrose: "No, and I'm not going to try it. I heard it was awful!"

Maryann: "Really, I went there and I loved it. I was hoping we could go there later, but I guess not."

Ambrose: "I changed my mind, let's go. I think I will like it."

In this example we actually see Ambrose making two Hasty Conclusions. He first accepts the negative opinion of James that the restaurant is bad without investigation. Then he communicates that opinion to Maryann. He then makes a second Hasty Conclusion (possibly because of an ulterior motive) to go to the restaurant based upon Maryann's experience and believes he will like the new restaurant.

IS/OUGHT NATURALIST FALLACY

The Is/Ought or Naturalistic Fallacy occurs when a person comes to a conclusion about the way things ought to be on the basis of how things are or are assumed to be. It is coming to an "ought" from an "is." Unfortunately this is a very common fallacy that is used by people to justify everything from the use of hymnals in our churches to acting selfishly in our decision-making.

Example #1 –

Pastor: "This Sunday we are going to be led in worship by our youth group. They won't be using the hymnals as we usually do, but they will be leading us in praise and worship using a PowerPoint presentation. The words will be on the screen for us to follow along."

Deacon: "Pastor, I don't think it's right to sing these new praise and worship songs."

Pastor: "How come?"

Deacon: "Well, we've never done it any other way. It's just not right."

In this case, no good reasons were given not to sing praise and worship songs other than tradition. It was assumed that something ought to be continued because of the way that it is.

Example #2 – An anthropologist might argue that imposing one culture's ethic on another is unethical. What if a culture practices racism by systematically killing another race of people who live within their cultural territory? Should it be assumed that because racism is practiced that it ought to be practiced without outside pressure to change? We hope not. However, this fallacy has also been used within our country to support racist ideas. Have you ever heard someone spout racist comments and when challenged their argument becomes, "That's just the way it is." That may be the way it is, but we do not believe it is the way it ought to be.

OVERGENERALIZATION FALLACY

An Overgeneralization argument is when a judgment is made about an entire group of people based upon the behavior, usually undesirable, of a few in that group. This is also known more popularly as stereotyping. Stereotypes are overgeneralizations that can become assumptions and shared by many people and at times, an entire group. Some stereotypes are of things such as public education, modern music, the arts, churches, synagogues or mosques. Other examples of stereotypes include people such as politicians, televangelists, feminists, athletes and blondes. People develop stereotypes when they are unwilling or not capable of gathering accurate information needed to make a fair judgment about a person or an entire group of people. Stereotypes can be very destructive to individuals and to groups of people. Overgeneralization or stereotyping should be avoided (as we would not agree with any of these scenarios).

Example #1 – "All homeless people are lazy. They just want a hand-out. If our city is ever going to be safe, we need to take drastic measures and send all of these homeless people to another city." In this example, an entire segment of the population is being labeled as lazy. In times of economic hardship, there are many who have lived above their means and now are in a state they never would have believed they would be in. A critical thinker could easily identify this as a fallacy of thinking.

Example #2 – "All Christians are hypocrites." It is often assumed that because Christians commit sins of commission and omission that they are hypocrites. However, this is due to a misunderstanding of both words—hypocrite and Christian. A hypocrite is a person who pretends to be one thing when he or she is actually another, or it's one who acts contrary to their stated beliefs. A hypocrite is defined as an actor who plays a role. A Christian, however, is a person who has been born again (John 3), or is one who has been saved by the grace of God (Ephesians 2:8). The point of confusion occurs because those who are accusing Christians of being hypocrites do not realize that the Bible clearly states that Christians still do sin (1 John 1:8). A Christian is hypocritical, however, when he or she claims not to participate in a particular sin when in reality they do. In that case, Christians are pretending to be something that they are not, and that behavior warrants the label "hypocrite."

To eliminate stereotypes from our thinking can be challenging. We must be aware of the stereotypes that are evident in our own thinking and challenge ourselves and others to eliminate them. One suggestion to get us moving in the right direction is to develop relationships with those whom we have stereotyped in the past. Progress may be slow at first, but it is well worth the effort.

OVERSIMPLIFICATION FALLACY

An Oversimplification argument is to conclude that an effect has only one cause when in reality it is the result of multiple causes. It is also ignoring the complexity of the issue and omitting other vital information to draw a conclusion. Unfortunately, this type of fallacy is used by some individuals when people are asking legitimate questions about why something tragic has occurred. It can also be used in everyday reasoning about common situations.

Example #1 – "Can you believe the shooting that took place at school yesterday? It was tragic that so many innocent lives were killed. How could something like this occur in our town? If gun laws were stricter this wouldn't have happened."

Regardless of your opinion about gun laws, this is an example of an oversimplification fallacy. It might be one reason that the killings occurred but unless further information is gathered, the issue is too complex for one reason to be given. More than likely the shooting was the result of multiple causes. What other reasons might be given for this incident? Be careful when making a judgment about why something occurred. There are usually many reasons to consider.

Example #2 –

Jim:"I just can't understand why my wife Mary thinks she has it so tough."

Dan: "What do you mean, Jim?

Jim: "She's a stay-at-home mom with three kids. How easy is that? I wish I could stay home and not have to work."

Can you see the oversimplification in this dialog? Have you ever heard this argument before? Clearly there are multiple responsibilities that need to be considered for a stay-at-home mom, and if Jim doesn't understand the work of his wife Mary, we are sure she would be willing to allow him to experience them for a few days to gain a better appreciation of her responsibilities!

RED HERRING FALLACY

A Red Herring argument is raising an irrelevant issue to divert attention from the primary issue. This fallacy often appeals to fear or pity. The argument also can use guilt to manipulate others into agreement and action. It is often inserted into an argument to help a person win the argument without directly dealing with the real issue. It is irrelevant to the real issue at hand, though it may seem to be related.

Example #1 – "Euthanasia should be legalized in the United States. Americans are overburdened with the costs of health care. Everything from the cost of hospital care to prescriptions needs to be reduced. The elderly overburden the system." Can you see the Red Herring in this scenario? The real issue is the legalization of euthanasia. Although people may want their health care costs reduced, does that address the morality of killing the elderly? No!

Example #2 – Lawyer: "Joe may have embezzled fifty thousand dollars from his company, but can you blame him? Let me tell you about Joe. He grew up in a poor neighborhood and had little to eat when he was a child. His mother did the best she could, but when he grew up Joe determined that he would never be poor again. Joe didn't choose this life of crime. He is a product of his environment. When you gather to make your decision, consider his past and determine his verdict to be not guilty." Although all of us should sympathize with Joe's situation, his past is irrelevant in his decision to embezzle money from his company. But people can be persuaded by the argument to vote "not guilty" because of their pity for his past condition as a child. In reality, Joe's childhood should not be considered in the judgment of the jury because he made a conscious decision as an adult when he committed the crime of embezzlement.

SELECTIVE PERCEPTION FALLACY

Selective Perception which is also known as One-sidedness or Special Pleading is arguing a point by selecting and presenting only the evidence that supports one's current position or opinion. It omits the evidence against it. Selective Perception gives reasons against an opposing view without considering reasons for it. Have you ever had a strong opinion about something without really investigating both sides of the issue? Have you ever believed something so much that you refused to consider any argument which was against your beliefs? This is when Selective Perception occurs. However, we must be willing to investigate other possible conclusions.

Example #1 –

Cathy: "I was born gay."

Jill: "How do you know you were born gay? Do you have any evidence?"

Cathy: "Because I have felt an attraction for the same sex as long as I can remember."

Jill: "But there is no clear scientific evidence to prove that anyone is 'born gay.'"

Cathy: "Well, in my experience, it's true. And all the gay people I know say the same thing, despite what "scientists" have concluded."

Cathy is arguing from her own experience and those of her gay friends. Her argument is based upon her own personal experiences as well as those within the community of friends she has known. These may be real and meaningful experiences, but her argument is limited to one-side of the issue and rejects evidence to the contrary.

Example #2 –

Donnie: "Condom distribution campaigns in public schools only increase teen pregnancies and STD's. According to a study completed at Franklin High school in Jackson, Ohio, teen pregnancies increased 5% and STD's rose 12% the following year after the health department's condom distribution program began."

Kim: "But what about the studies which were done in other cities where the rates were reduced?"

Donnie: "I wasn't interested in those studies since they didn't prove my point."

This fallacy of argument often occurs when you don't take the time to investigate an issue properly and only investigate information that supports your current view. It can easily happen if you are not careful. This can happen in courses where you are required to give a persuasive speech. You have an opinion and you want to persuade others to your opinion, so you research data that will help you win the class over to your side. The question that you have to ask yourself is, "Have I investigated this issue properly, and am I being fair in presenting the issue?" Changing your mind about something can occur when the issue is investigated properly.

SLIPPERY SLOPE FALLACY

The Slippery Slope argument is used when a person argues against an action on the unsupported assertion that it will lead to a worse condition. An assumption is taking place. The argument could be described this way: A leads to B which will inevitably lead to C. Although there might be reasons why C in this case is assumed to occur in reality it is only speculative and can't be proven.

Example #1 – "I don't understand why you allow your son to play those military video games. It's only going to desensitize him and turn him into a violent man one day." Although some adults who have committed violent crimes admitted to playing violent video games as children, it cannot be proven that all children who play these types of games will be become violent adults. Although we might want to argue that way to convince children not to play them, it cannot be proven at the time that playing violent video games will inevitably lead to violent criminal activity.

Example #2 – "Pornography should be protected by the First Amendment of the Constitution. If we start down this road of censorship where will it end? Mark my words, we will be burning books one day and every library in America will be closed because its contents will be considered offensive to someone." Here we have a classic example of a Slippery Slope argument. The assumption is made that if one item is censored then all items will eventually be censored as well. But how can this end result be proven in advance of its occurrence? It can't, though it is argued that way.

STRAW MAN FALLACY

The Straw Man fallacy occurs when a person presents another person's argument in a weak, misrepresented, or exaggerated form in order to win the argument. The reason this argument is fallacious is that it is not representative of their opponent's true position.

Example #1 –

Tommy: "Mom, can I go over to Frank's house to play video games? I will get my homework done as soon as I get back home. "

Mom: "Not tonight, dear. It is a school night and your homework needs to be completed first."

Tommy: "You never let me have any fun with my friends. As far as you're concerned, I might as well be locked in my room except to go to school."

Tommy is using a Straw Man argument since he is distorting his mother's position. If it wasn't a school night and/or his homework was completed, her response may have been different.

Example #2 – Most evolutionists will argue that Christians who believe in a young earth and who believe the biblical account of Noah's ark are wrong because there is no way that all the animal species alive today could fit in the ark. This is a misrepresentation of the biblical Creationists' view. Creationists do not believe that all the animals that exist today were created during the creation week. Thus, the Ark did not have two of every kind of animal that exists today. This is due to a distinction between micro and macro evolution. God created the kinds of animals as mentioned in Genesis 1, and then the different kinds did micro-evolve into the various species we see today. That is to say, God created a dog kind, and from the male and female dog kind, all the breeds of dogs we see today came about.

What Creationists deny, due to the utter lack of evidence, is that dogs evolved into an entirely different organism over time. This would be macroevolution. By misrepresenting the Creationists' viewpoint, evolutionists construct a straw man which is easily refuted; they are trying to cast anyone who believes in creation as ignorant and unscientific, thus holding a viewpoint not worthy of consideration in society.

"IF ANY OF YOU LACKS WISDOM..."

It has been our desire in this chapter to provide our readers with the knowledge and skills necessary to make good decisions. Your ability to identify the fallacies in these examples of flawed arguments can help you make better choices. It is through this process of critical thinking that life's most important decisions can be made and significant mistakes can be avoided.

However, having said that, even with all of this information regarding critical thinking, we recognize that human knowledge and ability still has its limitations. When an important decision is looming, not only do we need to engage our human critical thinking skills, but we also need to seek wisdom from above. "If any of you lacks wisdom, he should ask God, who gives generously to all without finding fault, and it will be given to him" (James 1:5). Note how God gives us wisdom: generously and without finding fault. Sometimes God uses the Bible to guide us in our decision-making process. At other times He uses circumstances to show us the path He wants us to take. He regularly uses wise counsel from those who have earned our trust to nudge us in the right direction. Often He will give us the wisdom we need through the combination of His Word, our circumstances and wise counsel. Our Heavenly Father loves nothing more than for His children to come to Him for guidance, showing our desire to walk in His will.

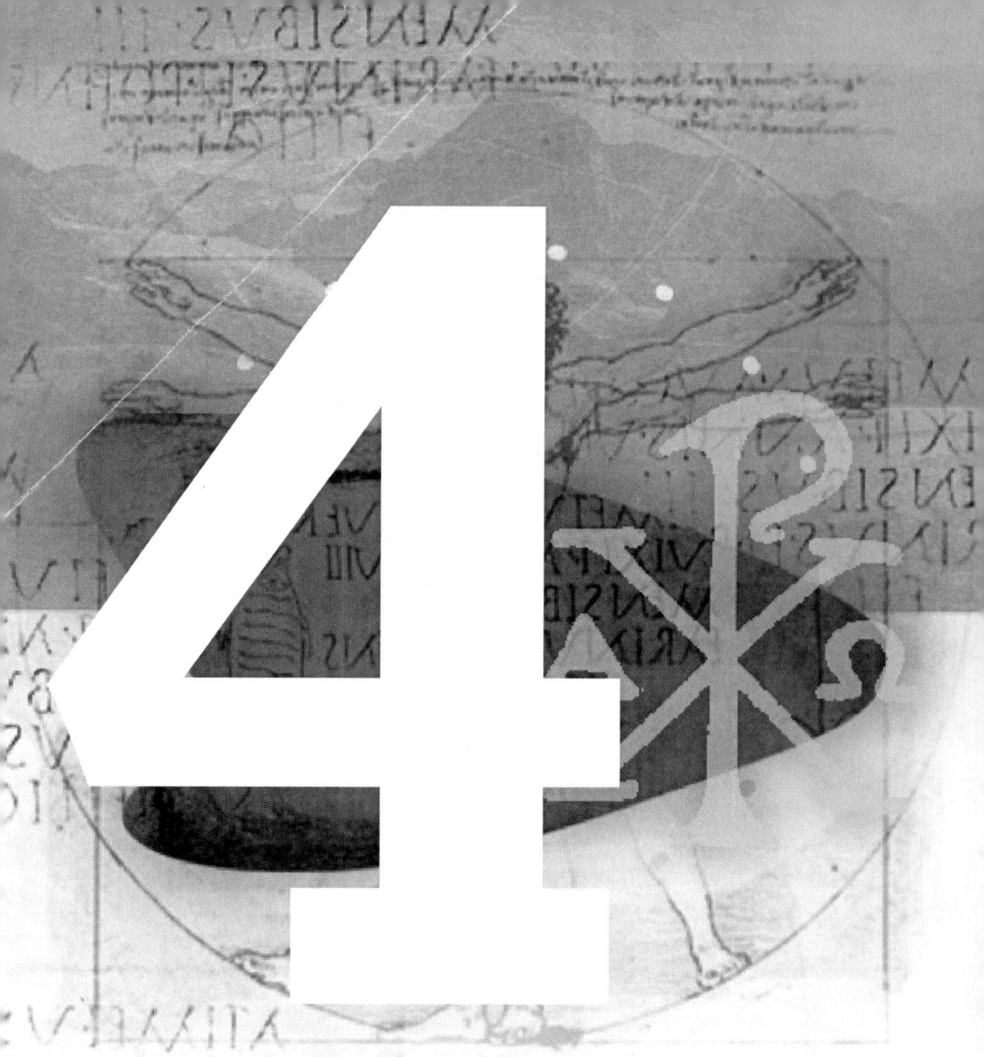

4

CHAPTER **FOUR**

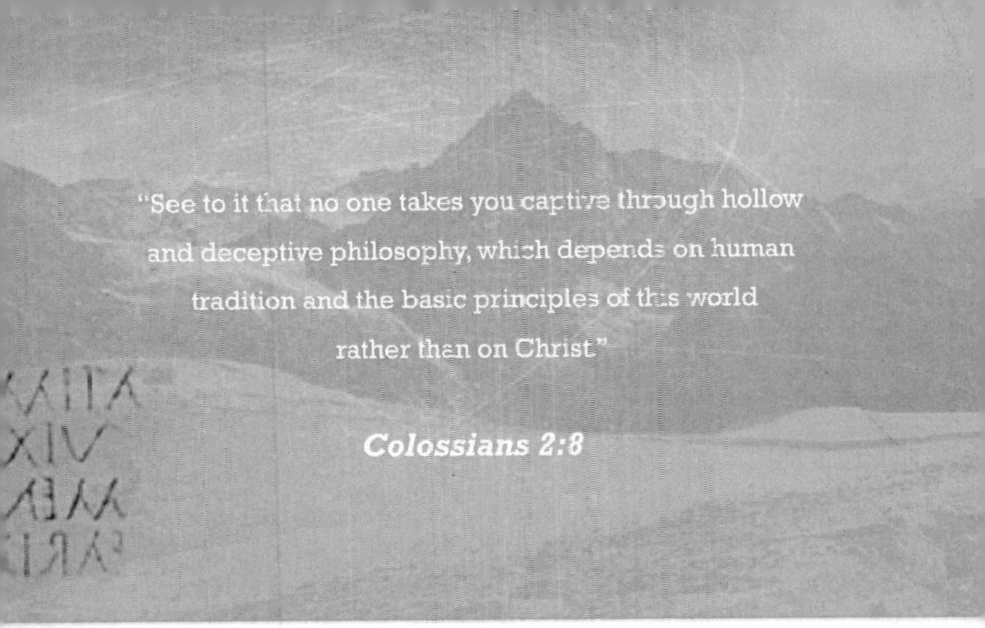

"See to it that no one takes you captive through hollow and deceptive philosophy, which depends on human tradition and the basic principles of this world rather than on Christ."

Colossians 2:8

WHAT IS A WORLDVIEW?

Have you ever watched a TV talk show or news program and after hearing some dialog you started talking to one or more of the panelists because you were frustrated at their comments? You knew that they couldn't hear you, but you still couldn't help yourself! At other times you might agree with the host or their guest, and you want to add your ideas to the discussion. Debates of ideas are often articulated in these formats, and they provide viewers with the opportunity to hear various sides of an issue. The debates are often the result of differing frameworks that people bring to an issue. Two or more people disagree about a particular topic because they are approaching that topic with a different set of presuppositions (things assumed to be true, partially true or completely false) and perspectives which can be described as worldviews.

WHAT IS A WORLDVIEW?

It is widely accepted that the term, Weltanschauung (worldview), was first coined by the Prussian Philosopher, Immanuel Kant in his Critique of Judgment, published in 1790. Weltanschauung was later translated as "our intuition of the world." According to David Naugle in Worldview: The History of a Concept, by the time the idea reached the United States in the mid-19th century, the word was translated in English as "worldview."

When you see the word "worldview" what comes to mind? A common response among our students is "a view of the world." Although this is partially true, it does not encompass the real meaning of the word.

There are many different ways to define the term "worldview." It is a word that encompasses a great deal of meaning, emotions, and potential consequences. Ken Hemphill in his book, Life Answers, says that "a world-view, whether Christian or secular, is the unifying perspective from which we organize our thinking about life, death, art, science, faith, learning, work, money, values, and morals. A worldview is our underlying philosophy of life." Hemphill focuses our attention on the breadth of the term. A clear understanding of our worldview will help us make sense of the issues we are forced to deal with on a daily basis. Some may say at this point, "Wait a minute, I don't have a worldview." It is important to understand that we all have a worldview whether we know it or not. We are not necessarily consistent or coherent in how we apply our worldview, but we never-the-less have one. We also use our worldview in response to the issues that confront us.

Chuck Colson and Nancy Pearcey in their book, How Now Shall We Live, describe a worldview as "the sum total of our beliefs about the world. The 'big picture' that directs our daily decisions and actions." Using their definition, when you are confronted with an ethical issue, how would you come to a decision about that issue? For example, if you were working for a company which markets a product and you were asked to lie about the product so that sales would improve, what would you think about that request and what would you do? How would you come to your decision? Would you be upset and question whether or not you should stay with the company, or would you lie about the product because you need the job. Would your perspective be, "Everyone lies so what's the big deal?" Or would you come to a different conclusion? How you think about that request and the decision you ultimately make, sheds light on your particular worldview.

In his book, The Universe Next Door, James W. Sire suggests that a worldview not only involves our thinking and decision-making but also the nature of our heart. According to Sire, "a worldview is a commitment, a fundamental orientation of the heart that can be expressed as a story or in a set of presuppositions that we hold (consciously or subconsciously, consistently or inconsistently) about the basic constitution of reality, and that provides the foundation on which we live and move and have our being."

A worldview, then, is a response of our heart or inner being; our intellect, emotion and will. It is the total framework we bring to decision-making.

A worldview can also be described as a filter or lens from which one sees and interprets the world and all that it represents. For example, imagine you are in a classroom that is divided into three sections. The professor passes out green-tinted glasses to the first section, blue-tinted glasses to the second section, and red-tinted glasses to the third section. She then asks each student to put on their tinted glasses and respond to a question. She holds up a white sheet of paper and asks each section to identify the color of the sheet of paper she is holding up. How would each section respond? The first section would respond by saying, "green." The second section would say, "blue." And the third section would answer, "red." Why? Because the color of their glasses affected how they responded to the question. In the same way, your worldview will impact your view about life's most important questions. Your worldview will impact how you view and respond to issues such as abortion, gun control, the origin of the universe, politics, and the list goes on and on. Another person's worldview will impact their answers to these issues as well.

So in review, what is a worldview? It is:

– a person's philosophy of life.

– a framework a person brings to decision-making.

– a filter or lens which a person uses to interpret life and the world around them.

DEVELOPING A WORLDVIEW

A person can develop a worldview from a variety of different sources. These sources may have different meanings and values to them and over time have varying levels of influence. Parents can be one of the greatest influences of a child's worldview. They guide their children during some of the most formative years of their lives. A mother and/or a father's personal beliefs and values are instilled and communicated to their children through their words and actions. These can be both positive as well as negative thoughts and actions that can shape a young person's life for years to come.

For example, a child who grows up in a Christian home may be influenced to become a Christian by watching their parents live out their faith before them. They go to church together, pray together and integrate Christian principles and practices into their daily lives. At some point, the child may make a decision for himself/herself and choose to be a follower of Christ and His teachings. However, if children grow up in a Christian home in which one or both parents are not living their faith consistently, they may become disillusioned about what it means to be a Christian. This could be the result of legalism within the home. Rather than the parents modeling a personal relationship with Christ, they emphasize that being a Christian is about living by a set of rules—rules that do not make sense to the children. But unconditional obedience is demanded by the parents rather than giving their kids permission to question and seek clarification about this set of rules. When legitimate questions are raised, the children are silenced or told to "just believe." Thus, they are not taught to think, but to simply have faith in whatever their parents believe. As these kids grow into their teen years they can become angry and rebel, leaving the faith of their parents for whatever makes them feel good or works for them. They have come to the conclusion, "If this is Christianity, I don't want any part of it."

The other extreme can take place as well. Parents can claim the title "Christian" but their lifestyle and actions do not reflect Christ. They may rarely go to church. Their home is not a place of worship, and the Christian worldview is not integrated into their life choices. Thus, the child grows up asking the question, "If this is Christianity, it is no different than the rest of the world, so becoming a Christian is meaningless." These scenarios can be true about a child growing up in any religious or non-religious home. Parents can have a profound impact on the development of a child's worldview.

Children and teenagers are also influenced through their friends or peers. Much to the dismay of parents, friends can have an even greater influence on their teenager's personal beliefs. For whatever reason, friends may seem to be more in touch with reality than their parents. They are constantly communicating with their friends through texting, Facebook, Email, Skype and many other social communication mediums. They are talking to each other and sharing ideas and beliefs, but those beliefs are not necessarily based on knowledge. That is why it is essential that lines of communication remain open between parents and children. Children desire meaningful communication, but they want to do so in a nonthreatening environment. They need to be led toward seeking truth.

Teachers in school can also play an important role in formulating a belief system. Teachers express their worldview through their course content.

Their personal attitudes and beliefs about a variety of issues surface throughout the school year. They can have a great deal of influence on children because they are seen as professional educators. As teachers build a rapport with a young person, their opinions are highly valued and trusted.

The media can also influence a person's worldview. Young people spend many hours a day listening to music, watching television, surfing the internet, etc. These mediums provide a constant barrage of worldview ideas, some of which can be confusing and create the idea that absolute truth does not exist. Ideas of right and wrong, true and false, become perplexing and in many cases non-existent. Truth becomes relative to the individual. Life can become convoluted and answers to life's most important questions seem to be evasive.

Religious education can also impact the development of a person's worldview. Because of the nature of religious beliefs and the potential impact they may have on life after death, a person can be highly impacted by such training. It can affect how they make daily choices, how they act, and how they treat other people. Many religions use sacred texts to guide their adherents to live a certain lifestyle. These texts can be a key source of information to inform the development of their worldview. For example, The Qur'an is viewed as the words of Allah and must be followed for a Muslim to potentially gain eternal rewards. In a similar way, the teachings of the Bible are to be followed by Christians. 2 Timothy 3:16-17 says, "All Scripture is God-breathed and is useful for teaching, rebuking, correcting and training in righteousness, so that the man of God may be thoroughly equipped for every good work." The Bible is to be used to develop right beliefs and actions, correct false ideas and wrong actions and to help a Christian be fully equipped to live a Spirit-filled life.

The development and change of one's worldview can take place throughout a person's life. Young people are not the only ones whose worldviews are impacted by these and many more influences. Everyone's worldview can be impacted, altered, or changed by external and internal forces.

THREE PROMINENT WORLDVIEWS

Although there are many worldviews which compete for prominence in our world today there are three primary worldviews that are most prevalent. These worldviews have influenced the development of other worldviews with variant concepts, requirements, and conclusions. These three worldviews are Naturalism, Pantheism and Theism.

Naturalism

This worldview begins with the presupposition that God does not exist, and therefore knowledge and existence must be answered in natural terms as opposed to supernatural terms and descriptions. Naturalism can be divided into two main perspectives, that which focuses upon epistemology (What is knowledge and how can something be known?) and ontology (What exists and what does not exist?). The basic tenets of Naturalism are that science is the source for what can be known and what does and does not exist. Only that which can be known through the senses exists. Mankind is autonomous, and yet through mutual cooperation and consensus progress can be experienced. Examples of worldviews which have been derived from Naturalistic ideas include Secular Humanism, Materialism and Nihilism.

Pantheism

For thousands of years various forms of pantheism have existed. Whether it is Hinduism, Buddhism or more recently the New Age Movement, all varieties of Pantheism involve reverence for the Universe rather than for any creator being or personal God. Pantheists deny the existence of a personal God. Their basic beliefs include the concepts that all that exists is a part of god, used in the sense that the Universe is sacred. Everything goes through a cycle of birth, life, death, and rebirth until one reaches a state of Nirvana, which is a passionless state of oneness with everything in the universe. Everything is sacred. There is a direct correlation and relationship between humans, animals and everything that exists.

Theism

Theism is the belief that "God exists." In particular, it is the belief that only one God exists. This God is usually personal and relates to humankind in an intimate way. Theists historically ascribe many attributes to their deity such as Omniscience (all knowing), Omnipotence (all powerful), Omnipresence (present everywhere), Sovereign (supreme authority) and Immutable (unchanging in essential nature). Examples of Theistic worldviews include Judaism, Islam and Christianity.

HOW TO RECOGNIZE A PERSON'S WORLDVIEW

As a student of worldviews, you will find many different approaches to evaluating or determining a person's worldview. These approaches ask many good questions which help you to identify what a person believes. The answers to these questions will also shed light on a person's particular worldview. In this book we will suggest five key questions that can be asked to identify a person's worldview. These questions will be answered through the three prominent worldviews listed above to provide an example of how to recognize a person's worldview.

The Question of Origin

This question asks, "How did life begin?" and "How did mankind come into existence?" There are many different ways that this has been answered. Some have concluded that matter has always existed and given enough time and chance, the end result is what you see around you today (Naturalism). Modern science is viewed to have the answers to the question of existence and any thought of God or gods is rejected. Scientists such as Carl Sagan and Stephen Hawking have been proponents of such a view. According to the Humanist Manifesto II, naturalists "find insufficient evidence for belief in the existence of a supernatural." Atheists such as Christopher Hitchens, God Is Not Great and Richard Dawkins, The God Delusion also propose the idea that God is not necessary for life or morals, and the answer to mankind's existence is found only in nature itself. According to Naturalism, man is a machine, a product of deterministic conditioning. Man has little, if any real control over his or her existence, and when the machine breaks, life is over.

Pantheists claim that god and the universe are one and the same. Although there isn't complete consensus with followers of Pantheistic worldviews, generally god is not personal but impersonal. That is, god is not a personal benevolent Creator who cares for His creation and answers prayers, etc. Pantheism views god as an infinite, impersonal force. An example of this can be seen in the Star Wars series. This force is all around mankind, and it is only when one escapes the entrapments of this world and focuses on the reality of the force that one can finally cease the process of reincarnation and become one with this eternal essence or force. The Pantheistic god does not create or have anthropomorphic characteristics. Thus everything has always been in existence and is a part of god.

Theism contends that everything that exists, including humans, is the result of God, the Creator God. God is said to have created Ex Nihilo, "out of nothing." Although differing in their concept of His nature, God is the first cause, the answer to why there is something rather than nothing. For example, the Bible says, "In the beginning God created the heavens and the earth" (Genesis 1:1). Moses, the writer of Genesis under the inspiration of the Holy Spirit (2 Peter 1:21) identifies God as the first cause. The Psalmist, David, declares that God is his Creator (Psalm 139:13- 16). Most Christian churches teach that God is triune and all three Persons of the Godhead were involved in the creation of the universe and mankind. Jews and Muslims are strict

Monotheists. They believe that God is One and is the Creator, but any concept of a trinity is blasphemy to the Jews and Muslims.

The Question of Identity

This question seeks to answer, "What does it mean to be a human?" and "Are humans more important than animals?" Since Naturalism does not accept supernatural events, they conclude that mankind is a product of evolutionary forces. The concept of a personal God is rejected. Scientific Naturalism is committed to an empirical approach to reality and truth. They seek to discover truth primarily by observation and experiment. Scientific Naturalism uncompromisingly leads to a Methodological Naturalism which is the idea that the only method to understanding the nature of things is through accepted scientific theory. Thus Darwinism is often viewed, regardless of its flaws, as the only legitimate approach to understanding how mankind arrived on this planet.

Naturalism also sets up a paradigm for understanding mankind's relationship to animals. Since they purport that everything has evolved, mankind is simply a more sophisticated animal, but is not greater in value over the animal kingdom. Since man and animals come from a similar ancestry, mankind should not be viewed or valued as superior in species. Peter Singer, the Australian Philosopher and current professor of Bioethics at Princeton University was a major animal rights activist in the U.S. during the 1970's. His book, Animal Liberation in 1975 was very influential in shaping the animal liberation movement. In that book he rejected a new term that he coined "speciesism," which is the concept that mankind should be privileged over animals. He has also created a controversy over his ideas regarding abortion, infanticide and euthanasia. Singer contends in his books Practical Ethics (1979) and Rethinking Life and Death (reprint 2008) that children in the womb and those recently born do not possess personhood. In Practical Ethics Singer states, "Human babies are not born self-aware, or capable of grasping that they exist over time. They are not persons"; therefore, "the life of a newborn is of less value than the life of a pig, a dog, or a chimpanzee" (Practical Ethics, p. 122-123). Peter Singer and others continue to contend that life is not sacred. Since this is the case, these Naturalists believe that abortion, infanticide and euthanasia under certain circumstances should be de-criminalized where current law is in place.

Pantheists consider all life to be sacred or spiritual in nature. It is man's essence, or soul that is important to consider. Historical Pantheism teaches that man's soul is eternal and when she or he eventually reaches a state of Nirvana, their soul (Atman) will become one with Brahman (Hinduism's concept of eternal soul).

Pantheism customarily teaches a life cycle called reincarnation. A person's future state rests primarily upon one's good or bad actions in this life (Karma). Karma is basically the idea that "what goes around, comes around." Although significantly different in its application, its basic idea is similar to the biblical concept of sowing and reaping (Galatians 6:7). If you do good deeds then you will be rewarded, but if you do bad deeds the end result will be negative in your life. In Pantheism, good Karma results in moving one closer in a future life form to gain Nirvana. Bad Karma results in being re-born into a lower life form, extending the cycles of reincarnation.

Humanity is only considered as a higher state in relation to reaching Nirvana. Thus, humans and animals have a similar essence and should be regarded as partners in search of eternal oneness.

Theism views God as eternal and that mankind is a special creation of God. In Judaism and Christianity, God created mankind above the animal and man was created, "a little lower than the angels" (Psalm 8:5). Male and female were both created "in the image of God" and were given the responsibility to rule over the animals and to be their caretakers (Genesis 2:15). Although the earth and animals are not to be worshiped, mankind is responsible to take care of God's creation. In reality, Christians should be leading the charge as environmentalists and animal rights activists while at the same time appropriately reaping the benefits of earth for its natural resources and animals for food.

In Islam, mankind is also a separate creation from animals, and Adam and Eve are real people created by Allah. Adam was first created. "He began the creation of man from clay, and made his progeny from a quintessence of fluid" (Qur'an, 32:7- 8). Eve is said to have come from Adam, "It is He Who created you from a single person, and made his mate of like nature, in order that he might dwell with her in love" (Qur'an, 7:189). However, there is also some acceptance for an evolutionary creation. This is based upon the interpreted passages in the Qur'an. It can be argued that theistic evolution is a part of their response to the issue of creation. According to the Qur'an,

> What is the matter with you, that you are not conscious of Allah's majesty, seeing that it is He Who has created you in diverse stages? See you not how Allah has created the seven heavens one above another, and made the moon a light in their midst, and made the sun as a (glorious) lamp? And Allah has produced you from the earth, growing (gradually) (71:13-17)

Allah was ultimately in control and was sovereign over creation. It did not happen by evolutionary forces alone.

Animals are also not to be abused. They are believed to praise Allah though they do not do so like humans, "The seven heavens and the earth and whatever is in them exalt Him..." (Qur'an, 17:44). Muslims are not forbidden from eating animals. Though vegetarianism is practiced by some, it is not a traditional practice.

The Question of Meaning or Purpose

The question of meaning or purpose asks, "Why does mankind exist?" And more specifically, "Why do I exist?" These are some of the most fundamental questions which mankind seeks to answer. They are questions with significant consequences. The answers to these questions have enormous implications for our lives and how we perceive ourselves and others.

Naturalism does not have a real basis from which to answer these questions. If mankind is a product of evolutionary forces and not a special creation of God, then man's real purpose is ambiguous at best. How can something that evolved from the impersonal and insignificant and whose existence ends without significance (death is viewed as the end of life) have any significance or value in-between? That does not mean that many who believe in naturalistic theories don't try to explain a concept of significance. For example, Humanism sees mankind as a highly evolved animal and through reason can conclude that man has the right and responsibility to give meaning and value to her or his own life. This is accomplished through the development of ethical systems based upon human values. Man's value and purpose is seen in his or her ability to leave a positive impact on others and the world around them. But on what basis do they presuppose that man has any value or significance? Since man is a machine and ultimately not in control of what happens, life cannot have any real value or significance. Any notion of such is simply an illusion.

In Pantheism, man's purpose is to end the cycle of reincarnation so that the soul can achieve the state of Nirvana. Nirvana is not a "place" like Heaven, but it is a state of liberation from the bondage of this earthly life.

In Hinduism, life is to be viewed as Maya or illusion. Like a dream or a mirage, our life and everything around us does not really exist as we know it. An example of this concept can be found in the movie, The Matrix. Mankind's perception of reality is not authentic and to achieve oneness with Brahman, one must eliminate all desire and that which enslaves him or her in the cycle of birth, death and rebirth (reincarnation). The purpose of man is to understand that life and all that seems to be real is an illusion. Man needs to understand this as quickly as possible so that this cycle can end. What keeps man in this cycle is known as Karma. Although good Karma (doing good deeds for others) can have a positive effect (can help you reach a higher caste system), it is still viewed as a curse since good and bad Karma keeps a person locked in this life cycle of reincarnation.

In Buddhism, life is not viewed as an illusion. One of the key teachings of Siddhartha Gautama (the one who became Buddha) is that suffering is not an illusion. Suffering is viewed as real and the source of man's entrapment to the cycle of reincarnation. The purpose of man then is to eliminate suffering by eliminating desire. Man should stop craving that which is temporary and follow the Four Noble Truths and Eightfold Noble Path to end all desire and reach a state of Nirvana.

Theists believe that the purpose of mankind is to know God. However, the way this is interpreted varies greatly within theistic worldviews such as Judaism, Christianity and Islam.

For example, Jews believe that man's purpose is to know God by following His commandments. Although there are several Jewish sects today, traditional Judaism teaches that man is to love the Lord and serve Him with "all your heart and with all your soul" (Deuteronomy 11:13) and to "love your neighbor as yourself: I am the LORD" (Leviticus 19:18). This is accomplished through keeping the commandments in the Torah, which are the first five books of the Tanakh (Hebrew Bible).

Christianity is about a relationship with God and not simply following the tenants of a religion. Religion is viewed as man's attempt to reach God. Christianity interprets the Bible as God's plan to reach man. The purpose of mankind, according to John 17:3, is "that they may know You, the only true God, and Jesus Christ whom You have sent." This is salvation in Christianity. It is about having a personal intimate relationship with God through His Son, Jesus Christ.

Muslims believe the Bible was corrupted and that God needed to communicate His plan for mankind through His final prophet, Muhammad. The Angel Gabriel is said to have communicated the Qur'an to Muhammad over a period of several years. Muhammad then communicated what he was told to his followers to write down. Mankind's purpose is to know that Allah is One and to obey the teachings of the Qur'an. This would include following the Five Pillars of Islam. According to Sunni Muslims, these would include:

– The Confession of Faith (Shahada)

– The Daily Prayers (Salat)

– Giving Alms or the poor tax (Zakat)

– Fasting especially during Ramadan (Siyam)

– The Pilgrimage to Mecca (Hajj)

Shia Muslims follow a different set of Five Pillars which is to be followed by 10 additional pillars. Islam is a works-based religion, so the purpose of man is to do enough good works in order to appease Allah and earn the right to enter Paradise and avoid Hell.

The Question of Morality or Ethics

This question seeks to know "What is meant by right and wrong?" and "How should I live?" If a person does not start with a presupposition that God exists and that He has communicated His will for man through some type of revelation, how does he or she determine what actions are right and which ones are wrong—if right and wrong even exist?

Among naturalistic theories there is no consensus. Most would fall into the category of Relativism. Relativism rejects the idea of absolute truth (something that is true at all times and at all places). Relativism teaches that truth is dependent upon the individual or society and is subject to change. What is right today may be wrong tomorrow. It is relative to internal and or external influences. Internal influences would be found in worldviews such as Hedonism, Egoism and Situational Ethics. External influences can be found in worldviews such as Utilitarianism and Conventionalism.

In addition, an Emotivist would argue that right and wrong do not exist in the way humanity typically thinks of it. When declaring that something is right or wrong, one is just expressing an emotion rather than stating a fact. One can see that diversity exists in Naturalism as to how these questions are answered.

Since Pantheism believes that everything is god and god is everything, morality and ethics (in a practical sense) are how one should act toward itself. This would impact how a person would treat other people as well as animals, insects, and plants. In Buddhism, Ethical Conduct (Sila) is taught within the Eightfold Path through Right Speech, Right Conduct, and Right Livelihood. However, man must look to the god within to determine what is right and wrong and ultimately the distinction between the two is uncertain. One must let go of desire and ultimately be freed from this mindset through mental discipline.

In Pantheism, man is autonomous, and morality is subjective and relative. Man's actions will return to him or her (Karma), and it is up to the individual to determine what those actions should be and how they should be carried out. Unlike Judaism, Christianity and Islam have specific absolute standards of morality.

Theists answer the questions of morality and ethics primarily through Special Revelation or their religious texts. Ethics is based upon the nature and character of God. Right and wrong are not relative to man's perspective, but are based upon God's holy standard. This is not to say that theists are consistent and always live holy lives. Jews and Christians believe in the fall of Adam. Adam knowingly acted against God's will by eating the forbidden fruit (Genesis 3). As a result, mankind is in need of redemption. How this happens then differs between Judaism and Christianity. In Judaism, man is in a right relationship with God through good works (Exodus 20:6). People are morally neutral with the capacity to do good or evil. Evil is defeated by observing the Law found in the Torah. Christians believe man is born a sinner (Psalm 51:5) and cannot save himself. The salvation of mankind is only achieved by grace through faith in the Lord Jesus Christ and not by one's works, but works inevitably follow true salvation (Ephesians 2:8-10).

In Islam, Muslims obtain salvation through their religious texts known as the Qur'an (primary) and Hadith (secondary). By studying these texts a Muslim lives a moral life. Hammudah Abdlati in his book, Islam in Focus, articulates Islamic morality by stating:

> The concept of morality in Islam centers around certain basic beliefs and principles. Among these are the following: (1) God is the Creator and Source of all goodness, truth and beauty. (2) Man is a responsible, dignified, and honorable agent of his Creator. (3) God has put everything in the heavens and the earth in the service of mankind. (4) By His mercy and wisdom, God does not expect the impossible from man or hold him accountable for anything beyond his power. Nor does God forbid man to enjoy the good things of life. (5) Moderation, practicality, and balance are the guarantees of high integrity and sound morality. (6) All things are permissible in principle except what is singled out as forbidden, which must be avoided. (7) Man's ultimate responsibility is to God and his highest goal is the pleasure of his Creator. (p.40)

Following the Five Pillars, as mentioned earlier, is essential to right living as a Muslim. These Pillars must be obeyed if one is going to live a moral life before Allah, and based upon Allah's decision a Muslim may enter paradise upon death.

The Question of Destiny

This final question asks, "Is there life after death?" "What will happen to me when I die?" "Will I have to answer for the choices I made and how I lived my life?" The answers to these questions can have immediate results as well as eternal consequences. Your worldview can affect how you act on a daily basis and direct the legacy that you leave behind. It can also potentially influence your eternal state.

The Naturalist is not concerned about life after death since death is final. When a person dies the material stops functioning as it did, and the process of decomposition begins to take place. Only what one has done to impact the lives of others and the world around them lives on. And that can and does impact some within this worldview. Community service, philanthropy, environmentalism and other types of meaningful activity become the naturalist's heritage in which the planet and people will be impacted after they are gone.

Other Naturalists such as Determinists and Nihilists have come to the conclusion that they have little, if anything, to do personally with the choices they make. Life ultimately is meaningless. Since life is meaningless the real question that needs to be answered is, "Why am I alive?" Unfortunately, some who hold this view cannot handle their concept of reality and attempt to mask the pain through pain killers, cutting, drugs, sex, alcohol and other addictive behaviors. When these are not enough to ease the pain, some end their lives. Death becomes the ultimate escapism.

Pantheists are very interested in answering these questions because they want to end the cycle of reincarnation. They believe that the choices they make while on this earth will have a direct effect on their future eternal state.

Hindus believe that one's Karma determines the caste you enter at re-birth. As an example, if a person has bad Karma it will result in being reborn into a lower caste or even worse, as an animal. It is only when one reaches the highest caste, the Brahman, which is comprised of religious teachers and nobility, that one has the greatest chance of reaching Nirvana.

Siddhartha Gautama (Buddha) rejected the caste system he grew up with, and he declared that everyone had an equal chance of reaching Nirvana. He retained the concept of Karma and believed through good Karma and the denial of desire one could enter the state of Nirvana. They would then leave the bondage of this world and enter a passionless state where one feels neither love nor hate. Nirvana literally means "extinction" which is the summation of a Pantheist's struggle.

Theists also consider these questions to be vitally important within their worldview concept. In many Jewish sects, one's eternal state is dependent upon faith and good works. How a Jewish person lives their life and the choices they make are essential ingredients which impact eternity. Salvation or saved are not terms that a Jewish person would use to describe their current or future state. They believe they are already the chosen ones of God and have been saved through divine preference. Their current standing with God then is directly impacted by their choice to follow the Holy Scriptures and that which He has prescribed for them to follow.

Christians believe in two eternal states for all human beings: Heaven or Hell. Heaven and Hell are both literal places where people exist eternally either in the presence and blessings of God in Heaven (Revelation 21:1-7) or in a state of separation from God, being punished in Hell (Revelation 20:11-15). The choice of receiving Christ as one's Savior or not making that choice while on this earth determines a person's eternal state.

Christians view good works as a result of their salvation (Ephesians 2:10) and not as a means to it. Good works are seen as the evidence of an internal change of heart. How a Christian lives their life reveals their spiritual condition. Jesus uses the analogy of fruit in John 15 to describe how good works occur. Followers of Christ who are connected to the Vine (Jesus) bear fruit (good works). Those who are not connected to Christ do not bear fruit and are cast away like a dead branch and thrown into the fire (John 15:1-6). What will happen after death is dependent upon a person's choices and their personal relationship with God.

Muslims also view two eternal states called Paradise and Hell. Paradise is gained by doing more good works than bad, thus salvation is based upon human effort. The Muslim view of paradise is ultimately indescribable pleasure. Following the Five Pillars of Islam, mentioned earlier, is essential to gain eternal rewards. Ultimately though, Allah is sovereign and controls the eternal state of humans. A Muslim does not know for sure until death whether or not they have done enough good to earn Allah's favor and enter Paradise.

If a person does not accept the Oneness of Allah and follow the teachings of the Qur'an, their eternal state is damnation in a place which can be understood as Hell. However, Hell has different levels in some Muslim teaching. The level of Hell one reaches is based upon a person's particular beliefs and lifestyle. For example, hypocrisy is detestable and Muslim hypocrites are punished in Hell. The most dangerous sin is Shirk. It is the belief in polytheism (belief in many gods), or the belief that God has partners (Qur'an 17:111). This would coincide with the Christian view of the Trinity. Muslims think that Christians believe in three gods and therefore, are polytheistic. Anyone who commits the sin of Shirk will receive intense punishment in Hell.

There is a great deal of diversity in the answers to these five questions. Although the responses you hear from a person may not be consistent, they become an important guide to knowing and understanding a person's worldview. Understanding a person's worldview can help you communicate with them better as well as help you understand what they believe and why they act in a certain way.

From a Christian worldview perspective, understanding the differences in worldviews can also aid in evangelism. When a Christian meets a non-Christian and they know and understand the framework of where the non-believer is coming from (worldview), it can help the Christian know how to share their faith using the appropriate approach with love and care. It can also help the Christian to fulfill the Scriptures. Specifically we are to "Always be prepared to give an answer to everyone who asks you to give the reason for the hope that you have. But do this with gentleness and respect" (1 Peter 3:15). We should be able to articulate what we believe and why we believe. The "defense" spoken of here is the apologetic approach we will use to communicate the truth of Christianity with those who are desperately seeking the truth.

WHY SHOULD YOU CARE?

At the beginning of this chapter we addressed the issue of a conflict of ideas. Those conflicts often occur because of the framework (worldview) that individuals come from which affects their beliefs. However, worldviews not only affect a person's beliefs but these beliefs can also affect their actions. That is why it is important for you to know not only what you believe but why you believe it and to challenge others to do the same.

Have you ever heard someone say, "Live and let live?" That sounds like a very kind approach to humanity. To say that everyone should believe and do what is in their best interest as long as it doesn't hurt anyone else seems refreshing and tolerant. However, because we are not isolated from others, and we live in community, how can a person's actions only impact themselves?

Our health care system is an example of why this idea just doesn't work. If a person chooses to eat or drink whatever they want and as much as they want, they might become ill. If they become ill and need medical attention, then their private actions potentially impact insurance rates and/or our health care system. Can a person's private actions have the potential to impact others? Yes, absolutely!

Think about it. How many ways can a person's worldview positively or negatively impact themselves and others around them? History can provide a plethora of examples of how worldviews positively and negatively impacted individuals, communities, nations and the world. Worldviews can make an enormous impact and by studying them it can help you to identify a worldview worth embracing and a worldview worth sharing with others.

As we have stated, your worldview is the framework upon which you base each and every decision that you make on any given day—whether or not you realize it. In this chapter we have looked at three prominent worldviews and how each one of them answers a few specific questions. With that background, the next step is to further investigate the Biblical/ Christian Worldview. What is it? Is it a valid worldview? Does it stand up

5

CHAPTER FIVE

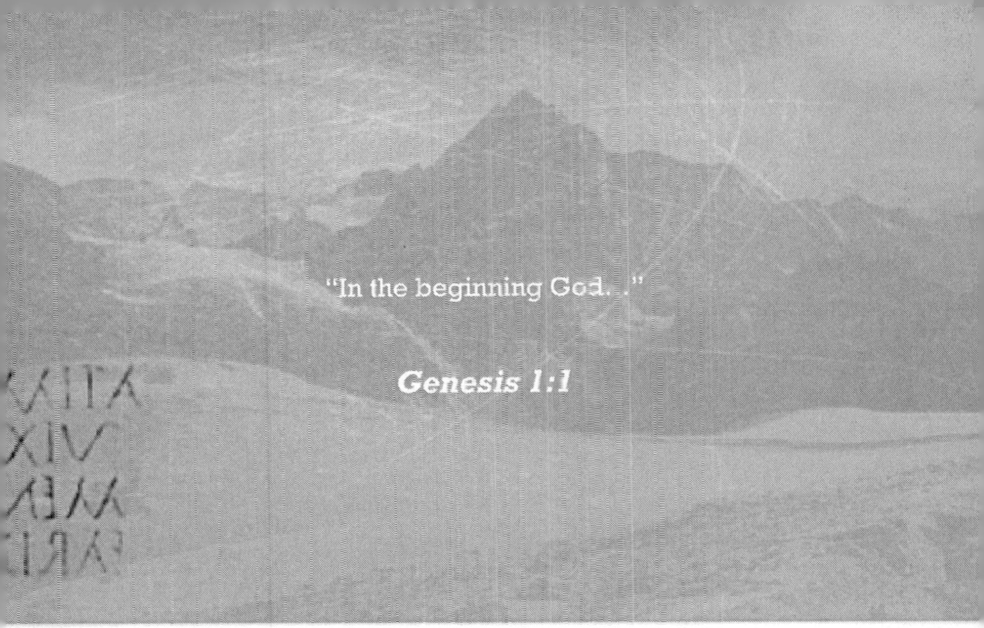

"In the beginning God. . ."

Genesis 1:1

WHAT IS A BIBLICAL WORLDVIEW?

HISTORY: THE GOOD, THE BAD, AND THE UGLY

A worldview is your philosophy of life. It is the framework you bring to decision-making. Each of us comes to a decision with certain presuppositions (something you assume to be true from which you begin your thinking). An atheist would have the presupposition that God does not exist and formulates his or her decision-making based upon that basic background belief. A Christian begins with the presupposition that God exists. The Biblical/Christian worldview begins with God who can be known through His creation of and revelation to humankind.

There are many good approaches to communicating the Biblical/ Christian worldview. At the outset, it is important to define the terms we are using. The term "Biblical" is added as a descriptor to indicate the lens or filter that will be used to formulate this worldview. We believe the Bible is the inerrant, inspired Word of God. It is the text that will be used throughout this chapter. The term Christian is used to identify the specific religious approach we are taking as opposed to other religious groups who also use parts of or the entire Bible in the formulation of their worldview.

History is a story of God and His creativeness and interaction with humans. It reveals the good, the bad, and the ugly way humans have responded to their Creator, and the story continues in all of our lives as we respond to His revelation.

This revelation of God to man can be described in two specific ways: general revelation and special revelation. Humans are incapable of knowing and being in relationship with God apart from His revelation. That is because humans are finite beings and God is infinite. God wants to be in relationship with His image bearers, and He reveals Himself to them through these methods. General revelation is God manifesting Himself at all times and in all places to all people. Special revelation has occurred in special unique times to specific persons in various ways. Today, this occurs through the knowledge of His Word, the Bible.

GENERAL REVELATION

God can be known in a general way by humans through two primary methods: nature, and the creation of men and women as His image bearers. David, the psalmist said, "The heavens declare the glory of God; the skies proclaim the work of his hands. Day after day they pour forth speech; night after night they display knowledge. There is no speech or language where their voice is not heard." (Psalm 19:1-3). The Apostle Paul also added this commentary, "For since the creation of the world God's invisible qualities-his eternal power and divine nature have been clearly seen, being understood from what has been made, so that men are without excuse " (Romans 1:20). According to these and other passages, God has made Himself known in a general way which should cause humans to further investigate His revelation.

The second method of general revelation God has used to manifest Himself is through His unique creation of men and women as His image bearers. We see evidence of this in four distinct ways. First, one can see evidence of God in the conduct of people which is distinct from the animal kingdom. Romans 2:14 says, "Indeed, when Gentiles, who do not have the law, do by nature things required by the law, they are a law for themselves, even though they do not have the law." Why do humans act in a moral way at all? Although deficient by the fall, it comes from being created in His image.

Another way we can see the evidence of God in creating men and women as image bearers is through our conscience. Paul says in Romans 2:15, ". . . since they show that the requirements of the law are written on their hearts, their consciences also bearing witness, and their thoughts now accusing, now even defending them." Why do humans even have a conscience? Scientists debate over the influence of nature and nurture. God has placed that inward faculty (conscience) in all of humanity, which pronounces judgment upon our attitudes and actions as being either right or wrong, and prompts us to do that which is right. Again though, this faculty has been impacted negatively by sin and cannot be fully trusted. Nevertheless, it does exist and cannot be ignored. T

The third way is evidenced through human codes. Although moral diversity exists between cultures, a study of "the golden rule" gives evidence that this moral concept has been taught by various religious and moral teachers throughout history. From Confucius to Buddha and from Jesus to Plato, the treatment of others has been communicated in a similar fashion. How could this similar moral concept be taught in such diverse cultures?

The fourth way is evidenced by human conflicts. This was previously addressed in Chapter 3. What is the first thing you assume when you are in an argument with another person? Did you say, "I'm right."? What is the second thing you assume? Did you say, "They're wrong."? If so, you have answered similarly to our residential students. Even by the nature of a disagreement, there is a basic understanding that someone or something is right and someone or something is wrong. More importantly, it gives evidence that there is a right and a wrong which ultimately originates in the very nature and character of God in His creation of human beings (for further study, see C.S. Lewis' Mere Christianity, chapter 1).

General revelation is limited in its scope. Because of the fall, humans were separated from God and limited in their natural ability to know and have intimate fellowship with God. Humans needed a final authority for our creed and conduct. God chose to continue to communicate with humanity in special and specific ways. What humans are incapable of knowing through general revelation, God has made known through His special revelation.

SPECIAL REVELATION

Special revelation occurs when God makes known vital truths which cannot be known through general revelation. Although we are limited in our understanding of God's relationship to Adam and Eve before their sin in the Garden of Eden, God was in relationship with them. Adam and Eve knew that they had the freedom to enjoy His creation, but they were not to eat of the Tree of the Knowledge of Good and Evil (Genesis 3). How did they know this? God had to reveal it to them. God has and continues to communicate truths to mankind through two primary ways: the Bible and the person of the Lord Jesus Christ (the Incarnation).

The Bible includes historic events in which God did the miraculous. He did some of these special things in full view of His followers as well as those who worshiped other gods. These events were then written down under the leading and moving of the Holy Spirit of God (2 Peter 1:19-21).

Some examples of these types of divine interventions include the birth of Isaac to the elderly Abraham and Sarah (Genesis 17, 21), and the parting of the Red Sea for the children of Israel, followed by the destruction of the Egyptian army who were in pursuit of them (Exodus 14-15). Other examples include the miraculous protection of Shadrach, Meshach, and Abed-Nego from the fury of King Nebuchadnezzar's wrath in Daniel 3 when they walked unscathed from the fiery furnace in which they were cast. "They saw that the fire had not harmed their bodies, nor was a hair of their heads singed; their robes were not scorched, and there was no smell of fire on them" (Daniel 3:27). The Bible also records that God spoke to individuals audibly as He did to Noah (Genesis 8:15) and to Moses (Exodus 6). He also spoke to men in dreams and visions (Genesis 20, 28).

The most significant method of God's special revelation to humanity is in the Incarnation of the Lord Jesus Christ. God "became flesh and dwelt among us" (John 1:14). The writer of Hebrews begins by saying, "In the past God spoke to our forefathers through the prophets at many times and in various ways, but in these last days he has spoken to us by his Son" (Hebrews 1:1-2).

Jesus Christ made it clear when He said, "He who has seen Me has seen the Father" (John 14:9). This was made evident through His unique virgin birth (Matthew 1:23), His sinless life (2 Corinthians 5:21), His miracles (Acts 2:22), and most powerfully in His death and resurrection (Romans 6:9). Jesus is the Son of God and God the Son. Here God's revelation is experienced in Word and in deed.

God's special revelation is communicated to us specifically today through His written Word, the Bible. 2 Timothy 3:16 says, "All Scripture is God-breathed and is useful for teaching, rebuking, correcting and training in righteousness." The Biblical/Christian worldview then can be shared with others as a metanarrative. It is a story that begins with the creation of the world and the special creation of man in the Garden of Eden. It was a beautiful beginning that took a tragic turn when Adam and Eve decided to rebel against God's will. As a result, sin and death entered the world. The rest of the story is God's work of reconciliation and redemption of humankind. It is a love story. It is a story of God's love and grace to each and every one of us.

CREATION

"In the beginning God created the heavens and the earth" (Genesis 1:1). It all began with God. The Father, Son and Holy Spirit (the Trinity) were all actively working as One in this beautiful creation story. He did not create from matter that which preexisted. God spoke the world into existence, creation ex nihilo "creation out of nothing." God existed before anything, seen or unseen. The Apostle Paul describes the role of Jesus Christ in this story when he wrote to the church at Colosse. He said,

> For by him all things were created: things in heaven and on earth, visible and invisible, whether thrones or powers or rulers or authorities; all things were created by him and for him. He is before all things, and in him all things hold together. (Colossians 1:16-17)

God is not the product of man's imagination or the result of some internal need to find meaning and value to life. The Psalmist declared "By the word of the LORD were the heavens made; their starry host by the breath of his mouth" (Psalm 33:6). God in His great omnipotence created the heavens and the earth, and by His great power creation is sustained. While God is present and actively involved in this creation story, He is clearly above His creation and not a part of it, as in Pantheism. There must be a clear distinction between the Creator and the created. God is not bound by laws of nature, but He is sovereign over and autonomous of His creation. He is not governed by His creation, but He is independent of it.

The first chapter of Genesis provides a beautiful synopsis of the six days of creation. In six literal 24-hour days, God did this amazing work. In chapters 2-3 the creation story is retold, but with an emphasis on the creation and initial responsibilities and activities of Adam and Eve. Today, theologians debate the interpretation of Genesis 1-3. They attempt to put God into an evolutionary box that tries to accommodate secular modern science. As soon as anyone denies the validity and authority of Genesis 1-3, it undermines the entire Bible. If the foundation is destroyed, the truths described in the rest of the Bible are questionable at best. If one cannot trust God's Word in creation, how can it be trusted at any other point?

During these six days God created everything in the heavens, from the sun, the moon, the stars and all of the galaxies that astronomers and stargazers marvel at through their telescopes. He also shaped and formed the earth and separated the waters from the land. He created plants and animals as well as the birds in the sky and the fish in the seas. God looked at His creation during the first five days and declared that "it was good" (Genesis 1:4, 10, 12, 18, 21, 25). On the sixth day, God created man and woman and saw everything that He made and declared that "it was very good" (Genesis 1:31).

Everything that God is and does is good. The psalmist said, "You are good, and what you do is good" (Psalm 119:68). God in His very nature is good. There is no flaw or deficiency in His nature nor in His actions. If our interpretation of God's nature and/or actions is anything but good, it stems from our lack of understanding or knowledge. "For my thoughts are not your thoughts, neither are your ways my ways, declares the LORD" (Isaiah 55:8).

God is the source of all that is good, and His goodness can be seen in the beauty of His creation. To some it is best described in the vastness of a starlit night or in the intricate detail of a flower. To others it is seen in the grandeur of high mountains, oceans, rivers and streams. The beauty of God's creation surrounds us all of the time if we stop long enough to notice and experience it.

GOD SAVED THE BEST FOR LAST

The culmination of God's initial artistic activities involved the unique creation of humankind. The Bible indicates that it was the collective work of the Trinity. Genesis 1:26 states, "let us make man." God in perfect harmony formed man "from the dust of the ground and breathed into his nostrils the breath of life, and the man became a living being" (Genesis 2:7). The Scriptures reveal that God gave Adam the responsibility of naming the animals. Adam realized that for animals there were males and females, but for him there was no counterpart. God then put Adam to sleep and took a rib from his side and made woman (Genesis 2:21-22).

Adam and Eve were uniquely created by God. The rest of His creation was spoken into existence. Humankind was specially formed by the hand of God. In addition, the Bible says that "God created man in his own image, in the image of God he created him; male and female he created them" (Genesis 1:27). God declares to the rest of His creation that man was the only one of its kind. A creation made in His image with a body and an everlasting soul; a "living soul" (Genesis 2:7). Humankind was distinct from the animal kingdom. He was distinct from plants and planets. Nothing was made like Adam and Eve.

What does it mean to be created in the image of God? An image is not the original. Humans are distinct from their Creator. They do not share in His divine nature, but they are to resemble or be like Him in many other ways. First, men and women are to be a reflection of God to the rest of creation. They reflect God by sharing attributes such as speaking, hearing, reasoning, loving and giving. Adam and Eve were created with a perfect ability to express and share those attributes. Although as their descendants we have been impacted by the fall and may not possess all of the potential characteristics, we can and are to use the attributes we possess today.

Secondly, man is to live in fellowship with God. Adam and Eve had the unique privilege of walking and talking with God in the Garden of Eden until sin interrupted that intimate relationship (Genesis 2-3). By our very creativeness there is an inner longing and desire to be in relationship and fellowship with God. That was God's design. He wants to be in fellowship with you. That is why eternal life is defined by Jesus Christ in John 17:3 as: "that they may know you, the only true God, and Jesus Christ, whom you have sent." Life, eternal life, is to be in relationship with God.

Third, humankind is to act as His representatives and stewards to all of creation. Genesis 1:28 says, "God blessed them [Adam and Eve] and said to them, 'Be fruitful and increase in number; fill the earth and subdue it. Rule over the fish of the sea and the birds of the air and over every living creature that moves on the ground." Man is to rule and act as a steward over God's creation. "The Lord God took the man and put him in the Garden of Eden to work it and take care of it" (Genesis 2:15). A steward does not own anything, but he manages the property of the owner. God has put humans in charge of taking care of the planet and all living things. The Bible does not forbid man from eating plants (Genesis 1:29) and animals for food (Romans 14:14), nor using its resources (Deuteronomy 8:9). Nevertheless, as His image bearers, we are entrusted to apply His character to His creation and not misuse it.

But why did God create? It was not because He was lonely or that He needed anything. It is a part of God's nature to be creative. He is the divine Creator. It was His will to create. The Apostle John declared in Revelation 4:11, "You are worthy, our Lord and God, to receive glory and honor and power; for You created all things, and by Your will they were created and have their being." He also wanted to express love to His creation. God is love (1 John 4:8), and He expresses that love through His goodness to man (James 1:17). As the Westminster Short Catechism states, "Man's chief end is to glorify God and enjoy Him forever." God created man for His glory and for man to enjoy the blessings of God (1 Timothy 6:17).

THE CAPACITY TO CHOOSE

Everything was in place for man to truly glorify God and enjoy Him forever. However, God did not create Adam and Eve as puppets. He created them with a capacity to make choices. They were able to make choices that had good results as well as choices that had bad results. By creating Adam and Eve with the capacity to choose between good and evil, God had created them in love. True love must be freely given and not forced through creative coercion. Adam and Eve were given the right to reject God's love and His commandment not to eat of the Tree of the Knowledge of Good and Evil.

It was not a free will in the sense that it was absent from influence. God was there and He was in communion with them. He had blessed them and given them beauty to enjoy and all of their needs were met. But Satan was also in the Garden. At some point after the sixth day of creation, Satan rebelled against God and sin entered the world (Ezekiel 28).

In Genesis 3 we find Satan, speaking through the serpent, having a conversation with Eve in the Garden of Eden. He begins the conversation by questioning the Word of God. "Now the serpent was more crafty than any of the wild animals the LORD God had made. He said to the woman, 'Did God really say, 'You must not eat from any tree in the garden'?" (Genesis 3:1).

God had clearly communicated to Adam and Eve His desire that they were not to eat from the tree (Genesis 2:16-17). Like the temptation of Christ in the wilderness in Matthew 4, Satan attempted to trick Eve into ultimately denying the Word of God. Satan lied to her. He said, "You will not surely die" (Genesis 3:4). Eve and Adam decide to reject the Word of God and to believe the word of Satan. Eve being tricked by Satan (2 Corinthians 11:3) ate the fruit of the Tree of the Knowledge of Good and Evil, and she also gave some to her husband Adam, and he ate it (Genesis 3:6). Sin entered the world. They tried to hide from God because they saw each other's nakedness and were ashamed (Genesis 3:7-8). They hid themselves from God, but they could not hide from the results of their sin.

The consequences of this decision did not just impact Adam and Eve. It impacted all of creation, including everyone who would be born of man throughout future generations. Creation was impacted negatively by the fall. The Apostle Paul said, "We know that the whole creation has been groaning as in the pains of childbirth right up to the present time" (Romans 8:22). All of humanity would be negatively impacted by the fall. "Therefore, just as sin entered the world through one man (Adam), and death through sin, and in this way death came to all men, because all sinned" (Romans 5:12). Humans not only choose to sin, but all of humanity is born as sinners. David declared in Psalm 51:5 "Behold, I was brought forth in iniquity, and in sin my mother conceived me."

Immediately the results of sin were evident. According to Genesis, Adam and Eve hid from God when they were designed to be in intimate fellowship with Him (3:8). Adam, as the husband of Eve, would now lead her in headship rather than mutual selfless cooperation and love (3:16). Childbearing and work were also impacted by sin's curse (3:17-19). Although it is not clearly stated, innocent animals designed to be enjoyed by man were killed to clothe Adam and Eve's nakedness (3:21). Blood was shed because of sin. Here is the first biblical example of the foreshadowing of the innocent Lamb of God, Jesus Christ, who would have to shed His blood and die for the sins of the world (John 1:29). God's original design was stained and the need for redemption became necessary. As one reads the rest of the story of the Bible, God's love and grace are put into action. The salvation story of redemption begins.

SALVATION

The story of God's redemption is ultimately the story of God's free gift of salvation through His Son, Jesus Christ. Michael W. Goheen and Craig G. Bartholomew in their book, Living at the Crossroads: An Introduction to Christian

Worldview, describe three characteristics of God's saving work from a biblical worldview. They indicate that it is "progressive," "restorative" and "comprehensive." It is progressive in that it begins in the Garden and continues to this day. It is restorative in that it is about "reclaiming His lost creation, putting it back the way it was meant to be." It is also comprehensive. Although His main emphasis is the salvation of humans, all of God's creation is in need of restoration. "Simply put, salvation is the restoration of the whole of God's good creation."

REDEMPTION

Salvation is pictured many ways in the Bible through five key terms. They are redemption, regeneration, reconciliation, justification and sanctification. The first term, "redemption" means to pay the price for another's freedom. 1 Peter 1:18-19 says, "For you know that it was not with perishable things such as silver or gold that you were redeemed from the empty way of life handed down to you from your forefathers, but with the precious blood of Christ, a lamb without blemish or defect." Jesus Christ paid God's redemptive price for the sins of the world. "God made him who had no sin to be sin for us, so that in him we might become the righteousness of God" (2 Corinthians 5:21). God's plan of redemption was ultimately not fulfilled through animal sacrifices but by the selfless sacrifice of the Son of God, Jesus Christ.

REGENERATION

The second way salvation is pictured is in the term "regeneration." It means to be "born again." "Praise be to the God and Father of our Lord Jesus Christ! In his great mercy he has given us new birth into a living hope through the resurrection of Jesus Christ from the dead" (1 Peter 1:3). When Jesus was confronted by Nicodemus at night (as described in John 3), Nicodemus believed that Jesus was from God, but he did not know the way to God. Jesus answered him, "you must be born again"—first by physical birth and then by spiritual rebirth (John 3:5-7). Being "born again" is not some strange religious belief by some weird radical Christ followers. It is a teaching from the Word of God regarding a rebirth spiritually. Because mankind is born in sin, we need to be reborn spiritually to enter into the family of God. Keep reading and we'll explain how that happens.

RECONCILIATION

The third term is "reconciliation" which means to restore peace and fellowship to a broken relationship. As we have already seen, "When God created man, He made him in the likeness of God" (Genesis 5:1). But when Adam and Eve broke the one rule God had given them, their spiritual connection/relationship with God was broken. Their sin separated them from God. We read in Genesis 5:3, "When Adam had lived 130 years, he had a son in his own likeness, in his own image" (Genesis 5:3). From Adam's first son to today, mankind is born into Adam and Eve's sinful likeness, so we need to be reconciled, to be restored in our relationship with God.

Not only are we separated from God, the Bible describes our condition as being enemies of God. Colossians 1:21-22 says, "Once you were alienated from God and were enemies in your minds because of your evil behavior. But now He has reconciled you by Christ's physical body through death." God is Holy, (Isaiah 6:3) and sin alienates humans from God. Because sin separates man from God, sin is His enemy. Those who embrace sin are controlled by it. After Adam and Eve sinned, God was not satisfied with man's condition. His plan was to reconcile humanity back to Himself through His Son Jesus Christ. "For God so loved the world that he gave his one and only Son, that whoever believes in him shall not perish but have eternal life. For God did not send his Son into the world to condemn the world, but to save the world through him." (John 3:16-17).

JUSTIFICATION

The fourth term is "justification." Justification comes from a Greek word meaning to "declare righteous or holy." It has also been used to describe a person who was declared free from guilt in a court of law. Those who have been saved by Jesus Christ have been justified. "Through him everyone who believes is justified from everything you could not be justified from by the law of Moses " (Acts 13:39). Good works cannot save a person so that they can go to Heaven. "For it is by grace you have been saved, through faith-and this not from yourselves, it is the gift of God- not by works, so that no one can boast" (Ephesians 2:8-9). Justification comes by being justified by God; "and are justified freely by his grace through the redemption that came by Christ Jesus." (Romans 3:24).

An example of this can be found in the New Testament when Jesus was on trial. Pontius Pilate could find no fault in Jesus, and he thought of a way for Jesus to avoid being crucified. It was customary to release a prisoner, sentenced for crucifixion, during Passover. Pilate knew that the Chief Priests were envious of Jesus and that is why they wanted Him crucified. He assumed the people would want an innocent man released (Mark 15:9-10). But the Chief Priests provoked the crowd to release a known robber and murderer, Barabbas, instead of Jesus. Barabbas was guilty and his punishment was death. But against his better judgment, Pilate justified Barabbas and he was no longer under the penalty of the law. That is what happens when a person is saved (justified) by Christ. "For the wages of sin is death, but the gift of God is eternal life in Christ Jesus our Lord" (Romans 6:23).

SANCTIFICATION

The fifth term is the word, "sanctification." It is a word that means "to set apart." It suggests the idea of a person who is set apart from this world and unto God. The Apostle Paul describes in 1 Corinthians 6 some of the unrighteous actions of people. But then in verse 11 he says, "And such were some of you. But you were washed, but you were sanctified, but you were justified in the name of the Lord Jesus and by the Spirit of our God."

Sanctification includes the idea of a person being clean before God and set apart to do His will. People often believe that their sin is too great for God to forgive. This is not true. God does not want anyone to die and go to Hell. He wants everyone to repent and be saved (2 Peter 3:9). There are also Christians who live a defeated life as if their past sins hinder them from being used by God. "Therefore, if anyone is in Christ, he is a new creation; the old has gone, the new has come!" (2 Corinthians 5:17). Christians should not believe the lie that they are bound by their past sins; they have a new beginning in Christ. Then, once this new life is realized, they are to be partners with Christ in the process of reconciliation and redemption. (2 Corinthians 5:18-20).

CHRIST AND CULTURE

It is one thing to know the Biblical/Christian worldview, and it is another thing to live it within one's culture. It is important to understand that this worldview uses the Bible as its filter for spiritual and religious truth and practice. It is another thing to know how to apply that knowledge in everyday life.

In 1951, H. Richard Niebuhr wrote a book entitled, Christ and Culture that described the way Christians characteristically approached their culture. What was true then is still true today. Christians often do not know how to respond to their culture. Although greatly abbreviated, the following represents his basic conclusions.

CHRIST AGAINST CULTURE

One of the approaches taken by Christians is to be against anything the world has to offer. It sets up a false dichotomy between those who are Christians and everyone else who is worldly and evil. The Christian is to affirm his or her loyalty to Christ and reject the influence of the culture. It is clearly evident that culture in and of itself provides little value to living the Christian life. According to 1 John 2:15, Christians are commanded, "Do not love the world or the things in the world. If anyone loves the world, the love of the Father is not in him." The world is seen under the influence of evil and is to be avoided.

CHRIST OF CULTURE

This approach not only embraces all who claim to be followers of Christ, but it embraces the world as well. They do not see a tension between the Church and the world. They adapt to culture and imitate the culture in their style of worship and in their lifestyle. This is not to say that they are not followers of Christ and His Word. They are followers who understand Christ through their culture. They understand His Word best through an interpretation of cultural happenings. Christ comes alive when experienced through culture.

CHRIST ABOVE CULTURE

This approach views a blending of Christ and the culture. Culture is not to be viewed as completely evil, but rather that good works taking place in the culture should be emphasized. The culture is viewed as "both divine and human in origin, both holy and sinful" (p. 121). Christians who take this approach make ethical decisions according to both Christ and the culture. Adherents of this approach see a harmony and balance between Christ and the culture. They view the Bible as authoritative but laws created by man are also from God and are to be followed. However, Christ must be viewed above culture and when the two are in conflict, Christ must be followed. The tendency is unfortunately to conform to the culture rather than to conform to Christ.

CHRIST THE TRANSFORMER OF CULTURE

Christians are to be in the world but not of the world. This means that they are not to be transformed by the world, but they are to be transformers of the world through Christ. Jesus prayed to the Father and said, "My prayer is not that you take them out of the world but that you protect them from the evil one. They are not of the world, even as I am not of it" (John 17:15-16). Christ has called His followers to be "salt and light" (Matthew 5:13-14). God can transform a "human life in and to the glory of God" by His grace (p.196). Apart from Christ, humans are incapable of transformational living. "But with God all things are possible" (Matthew 19:26).

CREATION VERSUS THE CREATOR

History is a story of God and His creativeness and interaction with humans. And history reveals that not much has changed since the beginning of time regarding how we humans (finite as we are) respond to our Creator (infinite as He is). In this chapter, we have considered several ways God has revealed Himself to His creation, and how He has made provision to restore the relationship of His creation to Himself. Yet, throughout history until now, many still choose to worship the creation rather than the Creator. In chapter eight, we will be looking at other alternative worldviews that are ascribed to by many today. These alternative worldviews put their trust in the creation rather than in the Creator. But in the next chapter, we would like to share with you our understanding of the message of salvation that is provide solely and sufficiently by Jesus Christ to all who will believe in him.

CHAPTER SIX

"But these are written that you may believe that Jesus is the Christ, the Son of God, and that by believing you may have life in his name."

John 20:31

KNOW THE MESSAGE

When I (Ben) was young, I remember my father asked me to go fishing with him at a state park down the highway a few miles. I loved to go fishing, so we hopped in the car and drove to the lake. We got our fishing gear out of the car, walked down the grassy hill to a semi-hidden portion of the lake, and we began to "wet a line." On that particular trip, I specifically recall catching a ton of catfish. They were biting like crazy! They were biting so well that it seemed like they were on our lines before the cast ever made it into the water. It was a great day!

When we filled the entire cooler with catfish, my father told me to make sure the cooler had fresh water for them to breathe and stay alive during our 30-minute drive home. Right then, I asked my father what to me was seemingly a very simple question to answer – "Dad, how do fish breathe under water?"

"Well, that's a good question, son," he said. And for the first time that I could recall, my father began to stumble in his explanation. Until now, in my eyes my father knew every answer to every question about everything. I remember he said, "Well, they pass water through their gills, you see?" as he pointed to one fish in the cooler. "Yeah Dad, I see, but how do they breathe air?" "Uh, well, they don't... but the water passes through their gills and there are air molecules in the water that they pick up through their gills, you see?" as he once again pointed to a different fish in the cooler. "Ok, Dad, I see their gills moving, but I thought you had to hold your breath under water because you can't breathe under water, right?"

What started as a very simple question turned into a very detailed and intricate conversation. Even though my father had a difficult time explaining the intricacies of how fish breathe under water, there was no doubt it was happening as evidenced by the catfish staring up at us watching us ponder these truths.

The same scenario seems to play out when people begin asking questions about spiritual issues – "What exactly is salvation?" "Does everyone need to be saved?" "If so, saved from what?" "How did things get this way?" What seems like simple questions are, at times, somewhat difficult to explain, even though the reality is plainly evidenced in our lives. However, the possibility of these questions causing confusion ought not to keep people from discussing them because the answers to these questions will ultimately bring peace to the human soul.

We have shared some of the basic tenets of the Christian faith throughout these chapters, and we have asked you to consider various worldviews compared with the Biblical/Christian worldview. In this chapter we want to give you some specific verses that can be used to answer questions about salvation that are often posed—either to answer your own questions or questions from those you've had conversations with about spiritual matters. This chapter could be used as a reference document for verses that apply to frequently asked questions. Hopefully these references will be a helpful tool so you can answer those tricky questions like, "How did things get this way?" and "What exactly is salvation?"

Questions about salvation have been on peoples' hearts and minds for thousands of years. In Acts 16 we read of a jailer who was asked to detain the Apostle Paul and Silas in prison for proclaiming the good news of salvation provided through Jesus Christ. Around midnight the jailer and the other prisoners were stunned to hear Paul and Silas singing hymns of praise to God. The jailer was not accustomed to witnessing such expressions of joy, especially from two prisoners who had been publicly beaten and detained for their personal religious beliefs. This unexpected zeal must have puzzled the jailer. I wonder if he may have mentally engaged in the message of the songs that these two passionate Christian captives were singing.

As you read the story, you will note that while they were singing God miraculously liberated Paul and Silas and their fellow inmates with an earthquake. It caused all the prison doors to open and their shackles fell off. The jailer, amazed at the hand of God and grateful that the prisoners had not escaped, was led to ask a pressing spiritual question, a question that was weighing on his heart. He ran back into the prison, bowed before Paul and Silas and asked, "Sirs, what must I do to be saved?" Paul's response to the jailer is one simple statement, "Believe in the Lord Jesus, and you will be saved" (Acts 16:30-31).

WHAT DOES IT MEAN TO BE "SAVED?"

This is a very important question – one that has both spiritual and eternal consequences. Using the Word of God, we will find the answer to this question.

It is interesting that the Bible rarely provides a full teaching of every concept of a doctrine within one verse or paragraph. Rather, the Bible disperses the full teaching of a particular doctrine within a number of related verses. As a result, one will not receive a full, clear teaching of a biblical concept until all the verses related to a particular scriptural topic are researched.

This is the approach we will take in our journey through the Bible in search of a full and clear teaching of salvation. It may seem like an insurmountable task but don't be discouraged; it can and will be a life-changing journey for you. I pray you will be able to reserve some uninterrupted time to sit down to read and consider the Scriptures we will reference. They will speak profound, yet easily understandable truths that promise to change your life forever.

Perfect clarity is needed in order to cognitively know the facts as well as the volitional requirements of salvation that result in a saving knowledge of Jesus Christ. To begin with, every Christian needs to stand firmly on the biblical truth that Jesus is the only way to salvation.

LET'S TAKE A LOOK

Knowing that the following verses are taken from the very Word of God, let's be patient and careful as we look at the following biblical passages. They will either confirm our already-established salvation, or they will offer guidance on how to receive eternal life and peace with God.

Romans 3:23 teaches that we are spiritually lost and in need of salvation.

"For all have sinned and fall short of the glory of God."

This verse clearly teaches us that all mankind is lost. Every person needs to be saved because every person is spiritually lost. And, unlike being lost in a forest where you may find your way out, the state of spiritual lostness cannot be remedied by human means. Why? Because it is our very nature to sin.

Our souls are not lost because of the sins that we have committed.

Rather, we commit sins because of our nature – our natural sinful state. Unfortunately, we often hear folks share the gospel by saying, "You must be forgiven for the bad things you have done." No. Our souls are condemned because of our sinful state, which is present in all mankind at birth. When believers share the gospel, they typically refer to the fact that the listener has sinned, but the listener must be led to understand that we commit sinful acts because we have a sinful heart and out of that sinful core, we manifest our true nature. Even though a person may not feel they are a sinner in need of salvation, the truth is they are. One's need for salvation is based on this truth, and it is crucial to convey this truth to nonbelievers.

In our society, most people don't like being lumped in the same category with murderers and kidnappers. Furthermore, they see things like cheating on taxes, swearing, or telling little white lies as not so serious. But to God, sin is sin because it is a manifestation of what is at the very core of our being. If our gauge for holiness is to compare ourselves with other human beings, I am sure we could all find at least ten people who we would compare to very well. But the Bible teaches us that the true gauge is God's holiness, the perfect glory of God – a standard far beyond our ability to reach.

Romans 6:23 teaches that we deserve to be punished because we have a sinful heart.

> "For the wages of sin is death, but the gift of God is eternal life
> in Christ Jesus our Lord."

Because of our sinful state, we have earned God's holy wrath. Our culpability for our sin is likened to how we expect to receive a paycheck after we complete a job from an employer. Once we have performed our job, we expect and deserve to be paid. Another example would be a criminal who is caught for committing a crime, deserving his sentence to prison. Because of our sinful state, because we have "fallen short of His glory," all of the souls of humankind deserve to be judged by God and receive a guilty verdict from Him. Upon receiving this verdict, the human soul is promised to be the recipient of a very tough, yet deserved, sentence . . . unless we can find Someone who is able to take upon Himself the penalty for our sinfulness and satisfy the judgment of God, releasing us from having to pay the penalty ourselves. The exciting truth is that this is indeed possible, but first you must conclude that there is no viable way you can personally pay the penalty for your own sin.

Isaiah 64:6a teaches that prior to salvation, even our best deeds or intentions are ineffective to save, and thus any attempt to save our own souls is repulsive to God.

> "But we are all like an unclean thing, and all our righteousnesses are like filthy rags..."

Our righteousness, or good behavior, is as "filthy rags" in God's eyes. This means that every attempt to achieve salvation on our own is impossible. Every good deed, charitable action, thought, or even our sincere pursuit and intention, is unclean and unacceptable. To think that we could merit salvation by our own efforts is nauseating and offensive to the God Who is the only One able to provide a sufficient payment for our sin.

Even though an unsaved person can perform charitable deeds and express kindness that reflects Christianity, at best he is performing those actions while wallowing in a sinful state, a realm that is offensive to God. Therefore, it is not the actions that save, but the change of heart behind the actions that is required.

Unfortunately, sometimes people don't even know they are living a life that is offensive to God. They never realize that regardless of their culturally approved, or even church approved lifestyle, if their sinful state has never been addressed through God's forgiveness and cleansing, their actions come from a heart that is repulsive to God. For example, it would be the same as accepting the words, "I'm sorry, please forgive me" from a person who was in the middle of plotting their second attempt to steal your belongings. The words, if devoid of context, sound good, but they are not backed up by a heart that is pure and clean. Again, it is our sinful state that has earned us God's wrath and judgment and any "cleaning up" of our actions, words, or deeds without experiencing true heart change is, in effect, futile and powerless because it is done from a heart that is an offense to God.

Titus 3:5 teaches that there is no possible way to obtain salvation by our good thoughts or by our good deeds.

> "Not by works of righteousness which we have done, but according to His mercy He saved us, through the washing of regeneration and renewing of the Holy Spirit."

This verse illustrates that there is only One who provides the cleansing of our sinful state: God Himself in the form of the Holy Spirit. We have seen that we cannot save ourselves; we need God to save us. It is all about what God does in this one-sided process for us. This is further developed in Matthew 5:3, "Blessed are the poor in spirit, for theirs is the kingdom of heaven." We cannot bring anything of spiritual value in and of ourselves to the table that could positively persuade God to establish peace with Him apart from receiving His forgiveness.

When we approach the spiritual "bargaining table" with God regarding our salvation, it is actually a place where we simply plead with Him for His grace and mercy. There is no bargaining at all in this one-sided arbitration. We cannot approach God and say, "Let me remind you who my parents are," or, "Here is my stellar history of community service," or "Look at all of my accomplishments." There is literally nothing that we can put on the table that can entice God to say, "Wow! Now this guy really lived a great life. If anyone deserves heaven, it should be him!" On the contrary, Matthew 5:3 teaches that if you want to enter into the Kingdom of God, you must acknowledge that you are "poor in spirit," no matter what you have accomplished in your life.

What is interesting is that, in the original language of the New Testament (called "koine Greek," pronounced "COIN-ay"), there were actually two words for the word "poor" that the Holy Spirit could have chosen to describe one's spiritual state in Matthew 5:3. One of the words is the word penichros (pronounced PENnycross) which means that someone is "needy" or "poor." This would refer to someone who has some possessions but needs additional things to add to his collection of possessions (e.g. you have a car, but need gas; you have a house, but need food, etc). But that is not the word that is translated "poor" in Matthew 5:3.

The word used in this verse is "Ptokos" (pronounced "p-toe-COSS") which means "totally destitute" or "utterly impoverished." This word is used to describe someone who literally has absolutely nothing. This same word is used in the Gospel of Luke to describe a beggar who is extending his arms asking for alms on a street corner. Being incredibly ashamed of his destitute state, he chooses to hide his face in shame as he pleads for alms (Luke 18).

Therefore, Matthew 5:3 teaches that the one who approaches God and receives salvation has nothing to offer God in his attempt to persuade God to save him. The individuals who will inherit eternal life are those who come to God recognizing and acknowledging that they have nothing to change their sinful state. They understand that, without God's intervention, they ought to be the recipients of punishment.

As professors, we have no greater joy than to watch students grow academically, socially, physically, and spiritually. There are some students we tend to interact with more than others because they are enrolled in a particular training program. It is with these students that we have more occasion to "do life" with on a regular basis. Throughout the years, we interact formally in the classroom and informally in the office or hallway as we flesh out various issues, decisions, and challenges. Most of the time, these conversations are positive and amicable, but sometimes a conversation may be prescriptive or involve a soft reproof due to a recent poor choice or action taken by the student. It is never easy to confront a student and talk about their poor choices, but it is all a part of demonstrating to the student that we sincerely care for their well being, character, and testimony.

I (Ben) recall a new professor who joined our university faculty who asked me about how to strike the right balance in the professor-student relationship, and how to balance having a friendship with the student while at the same time reserving the right to correct the student, if necessary. I responded by describing how God deals with us as His children.

God loves us and wants the best for us. He lovingly maintains a standard of personal righteousness that is required of every person. God will not lower this standard because that would be a lie, and it would not be in the best interest for the person. Likewise, we as professors must confront only when necessary, always asking ourselves what is the best piece of advice for this student.

Then I told him that the way you know you have struck the right balance is when, at the end of their academic career, you have that bitter-sweet feeling of joy and sadness as you see them walk across the stage and celebrate the completion of one phase of their life. You know you have poured your life into them, you wish you could have done more, but you are thankful for the rich times you experienced together.

I instructed the new professor on one more scenario that he might come up against when a student he knows well confesses to him and admits guilt and responsibility for a wrong doing without making excuses or trying to hide the truth. I advised him it is at that point you want to show the student mercy and try to work with him, because in his heart he understands and accepts both the weight of his actions and the value of the mercy you will show him.

That is exactly what our Lord requires of us as we approach Him and acknowledge that we are "poor in spirit." As we recognize our guilt and our inability to rectify it, only then do we understand the true value of the mercy God lavishes upon us.

Ephesians 2:8-9 teaches that no person is able to boast about how they are able to save their own soul because salvation is made available in the form of a gift from God to all who desire to receive His salvation.

> "For by grace you have been saved through faith, and that not of yourselves; it is the gift of God, not of works, lest anyone should boast."

The Bible teaches that God invites anyone to accept His free gift, knowing that sufficient payment cannot be found within the power or abilities of the person who stands in need of salvation. This payment for sin does not spring forth from a heart that is tainted with sin. You cannot change your spiritual state by some deed or physical act. The best deed done with the purest of intentions in man's eyes will never be able to change his spiritual state of sinfulness.

I repeat, it is impossible to change your spiritual state by physical means. I liken it to when people get emotionally depressed. They just sit in front of the television or eat a gallon of ice cream to appease their deep-seated pain. The TV and ice cream may provide a temporary getaway from one's problems, but they certainly don't confront the root of the problem. Even Judas Iscariot, after betraying Jesus Christ and feeling a deep emotional regret, went back to the Sanhedrin and tried to return the thirty pieces of silver in an attempt to appease his condemned conscience, but his attempt was futile (Matthew 27:3-5). Regardless of how much we would want to save our own soul, we cannot change our spiritual state ourselves. Therefore, we cannot brag to others that we had any part in our salvation. "It is by grace you have been saved through faith," meaning that salvation is through trust and total dependence on God to save you. Salvation cannot be produced from within ourselves; it is a gift that only God can give you.

According to Ephesians 2:8-9, the payment for one's sin must come from a source that is holy, righteous, and absent of any sin whatsoever. It logically follows that the gift of salvation must come from the only One who is able to produce a pure gift to appease righteous and holy judgment: God Himself. Therefore, the One before Whom we stand in a guilty and sinful state is the same One we plead with to be merciful to us, to forgive us, and to extend His grace and divine mercy to us.

Romans 5:8 teaches that God extended an invitation for you to enter into a peaceful relationship with Him.

> "But God demonstrates His own love toward us, in that while we were still sinners, Christ died for us."

Notice that this verse begins with the word "but," contrasting any notion that we can save ourselves. This verse offers hope but not before we conclude that our soul is utterly lost and guilty in God's eyes. Prior to offering hope, this verse accentuates the impossibility of saving our own souls.

By now, have you noticed that the Bible wants to drive home the state of our lostness? Why is this? Probably because the degree to which we understand the depth of our lostness determines the degree to which we will value the gift of salvation that allows us to have peace with God. By understanding what the Bible teaches about our hopelessness without Christ, we realize that our souls need a merciful God to intervene in order to provide us the gift of salvation that we are unable to provide for ourselves.

It is indeed a scary thing to know that, aside from God's intervention, we would forever remain in our sinful state and receive eternal judgment. 1 John 1:5 says, "God is light and in Him is no darkness at all." As long as we have a sinful heart that has not been forgiven by God, we cannot commune with our Creator, the God of heaven and earth (Psalm 5:4). We cannot have an intimate relationship with Him. We may generally be aware that there is a "higher being" that is more powerful than we are, and we may even try to talk to Him from time to time, but we really can't have a personal relationship with Him until our sinfulness is dealt with.

Romans 5:8 adds an interesting glimpse into the gracious heart of God found in the phrase, "while we were yet sinners." The Lord Jesus Christ provided a payment for our sin even when we had no idea that we were sinners. Before we came to our senses spiritually, He had His hand extended to offer salvation for our sin. This is what should cause our hearts to grieve over a world of people who mock His name. They are completely unaware of what Jesus went through for them and do not realize that He is offering full salvation if they would only believe in Him and receive His free gift. It is sobering to know there are people walking around today that have physical, economical, familial, or political peace, but not peace in their soul through Jesus Christ. People's souls do not receive punishment because of a lack of an invitation to receive that peace, but because they will not accept Christ's payment for sin.

Romans 10:9-10 teaches that if we want to accept Christ, we must respond in TWO ways.

> "That if you confess with your mouth the Lord Jesus and believe in your heart that God has raised Him from the dead, you will be saved. For with the heart one believes to righteousness, and with the mouth confession is made to salvation."

This passage teaches us that we must respond in two ways. Responding in one way without responding in the other way does not result in salvation. Before we can confess with our mouth the Lord Jesus, we must first have a cognitive understanding of four facts:

1. Agree with God regarding our sinful state.

We must be in agreement that our sinful state merits judgment and spiritual death. We must concede that we deserve to pay the penalty for our sin.

2. Believe that Jesus is God.

We have to believe that Jesus is 100% God. If Jesus is just some man, then He is humanly unable to offer salvation. If He's just a good teacher, then He is unable to offer forgiveness of sins through His salvation. If this were true, He could only point you to a way of salvation rather than saying, "I am the way, the truth, and the life. No one comes to the Father except through Me." (John 14:6).

3. Believe that Jesus' sacrifice was the only sufficient sacrifice to atone for your sin.

We must believe that Jesus' sacrifice is sufficient in totality, and it is able to provide atonement for our sin. Atonement means to cover by virtue of providing a payment. Sufficient means that the atonement was not only paid in full, but it was the only payment possible to fully pay for our sin. In other words, we don't need anything else. Jesus Christ's death on the cross and resurrection are totally adequate to atone for our sins and our sin debt.

Again, the reason why Jesus had to die on the cross was because our sin debt needed to be paid for. Because God is a just God, someone was required to pay the price. Without Jesus, we are compelled to pay this eternal price ourselves. Prior to accepting Jesus Christ's payment for my sin, I was the one who, upon death, would have been called upon to pay for my sin. However, I applied Jesus Christ's payment to my heart and received His salvation, accepting His payment for the sin debt that I owed.

4. Believe that Jesus physically rose from the dead, thereby proving that He can conquer both physical and spiritual death.

Romans 10:9-10 says, "that if you confess with your mouth the Lord Jesus and believe in your heart that God has raised Him from the dead, you will be saved. For it is with your heart that you believe and are justified, and it is with your mouth that you confess and are saved.

In our finite human minds, we may not have a problem believing that Jesus lived or that He forgives sins, but it may seem difficult to fathom that Jesus Christ also arose from the dead. Fortunately, the truth of His resurrection is clearly taught and concretely defendable. In order to accept God's offer of salvation, we must believe fully that Jesus physically rose from the dead, and is alive and well in heaven today.

JUST KNOWING ISN'T EVERYTHING

Like I said at the outset, sometimes seemingly "simple" questions are weighted with great significance and meaning – especially questions that deal with issues of spirituality, one's soul, and the need to have true peace with God. This chapter has served to provide a straightforward explanation of some spiritual questions that everyone must answer in his/her life. Fortunately, the Bible offers some clear answers to these important questions. There is more to this spiritual discussion though.

Now that we know exactly what salvation is, it is equally important to know what it is not. Salvation is not just a matter of cognitive knowledge – knowledge alone is not enough. We'll discuss this further in the next chapter.

CHAPTER **SEVEN**

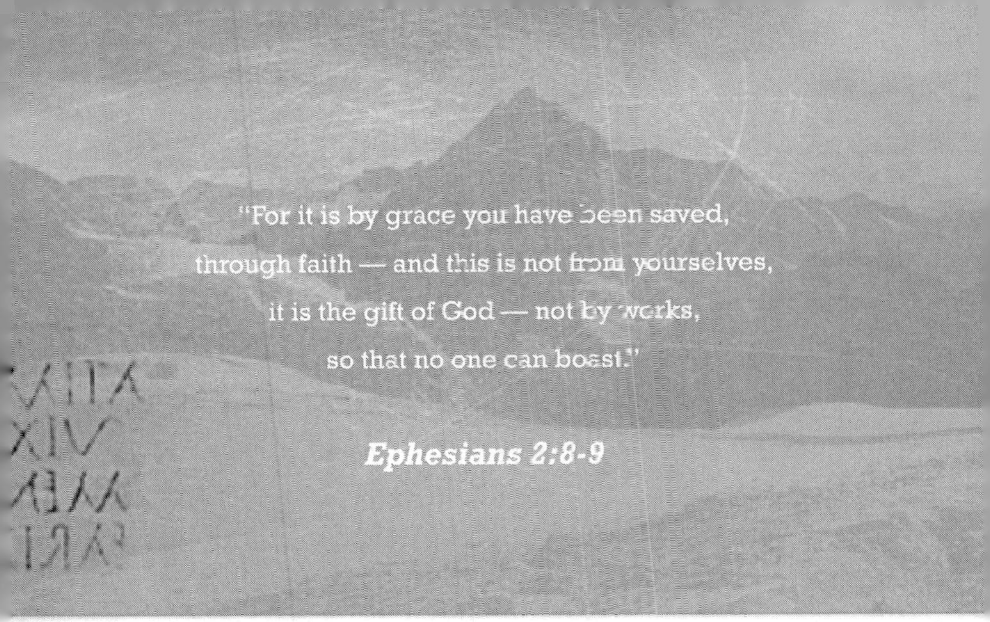

"For it is by grace you have been saved,
through faith — and this is not from yourselves,
it is the gift of God — not by works,
so that no one can boast."

Ephesians 2:8-9

YOU MUST BELIEVE

This may surprise you – for sure it shocked me when I personally contemplated what I'm about to share. The more I have searched the Scriptures, I have discovered a very distinct difference between simply knowing only the facts about God and knowing those facts along with knowing the God of the facts. There is an unmistakable difference between those two scenarios.

You may have read the previous chapter's cognitive facts and got excited about these great truths, but the key question is this, "What makes true belief in Jesus Christ any different from what the demons believe about Him? They acknowledge the exact same four cognitive facts about Jesus Christ that we discussed in chapter 6.

In the book of James, the Bible says, "Even the demons believe – and shudder." (James 2:19b). Further, in Mark 1:24 there was one encounter where the demons came to Jesus while they possessed an individual and one of them said, "What do you want with us, Jesus of Nazareth? Have you come to destroy us? I know who you are – the Holy One of God."

I would actually like to get some church members to say something like that on occasion. We know biblically that demons can never be saved because they are forever against Christ. They hate Christ and do everything possible to thwart the plan of Christ. But they believe cognitively every single fact we have listed about Jesus Christ. Demons believe that He is God, and they believe that Jesus Christ's sacrifice was indeed sufficient to save from sins. They also believe He rose from the dead. In fact, it seems they probably know a whole lot more about Scripture and believe it more than some professing Christians.

So, what completes the process beyond our knowledge? What is enough? After you die and you stand before God, what will you say when He asks you, "Why should I let you into My heaven?" Would you be able to express your answer to God as you stand in awe before Him?

The answer: A person must know the truths of Christ cognitively and believe them volitionally!

Believing volitionally is an act of the will. It is total dependence and trust in Jesus Christ. Willingly invite God to infuse your heart, which is the center of your decision-making force, with His purpose, truth and conviction. It is not belief in a creed or a mere belief system, but it is choosing to place your total trust in the Person of Jesus Christ. It must be more than the acknowledgment that demons give to Jesus Christ. The difference is in the heart's love and commitment to have Jesus as a welcomed ruler of your soul.

This is evidenced in Romans 10:9-10 where we see that when we accept Christ we are responding in two ways. The second way is volitionally – an act of the will. When we say that we "ask Christ into our heart," what does that really mean? When the heart is referenced in Scripture it often signifies thinking, not just feeling. "For as he [a man] thinks in his heart, so is he" (Proverbs 23:7, NKJV). Or "For out of the overflow of the heart the mouth speaks" (Matthew 12:34b). It's a mistake, biblically and exegetically, to say that the heart is the emotion and the mind is the intellect, because often in the Old Testament the heart is coupled with words that denote thinking.

When you speak of the heart, or when you accept Christ, it is more than a cognitive action, more than credence – it is dependence and full trust in Him. We literally ask and call on Christ to infuse our lives, our hearts and our thoughts with His will. That's why Jesus in John 10:27 says that a great evidence of salvation is this, "My sheep listen to my voice; I know them, and they follow me." Christians will not always have full agreement on all doctrines, but I know one thing: a person's good deeds or charitable actions will not save him; however, words, deeds, trust and attitude are all great evidences that you have accepted Christ. When you are saved, your life reflects dependence on Christ and commitment to His Word. You may not know everything as a believer, but you have that passion to grow. How do you know you believe volitionally? At the moment of requesting salvation, the heart will experience these realities:

Your heart will have remorse over sin.

In Matthew 5, the Beatitudes passage, we read, "Blessed are those who mourn." After you realize that you are poor in spirit, you begin to mourn; it makes perfect, logical sense. We have remorse, not just because we are caught or enslaved by sin, but because we truly feel remorse over our sin and our sinful state. We feel ashamed of our sin and because of our lifestyle, we want to change our spiritual condition. It is through this remorse that we see our need for a perfect God.

Your heart will repent for your sin.

Repentance is more than feeling bad. Repentance is turning and running, going in the opposite direction. You are literally grieved and that grief has turned your heart to run to what is right and holy. Will we be tempted to turn around and consider our old ways? Unfortunately, yes. But there will always be some level of conviction after we sin because that behavior is contrary to our newly forgiven nature.

You will request salvation from sin.

A new believer's prayer sounds something like this: "I don't want my sinful state anymore. I don't want to function out of a state that is offensive to You, Holy God. Would You change me and give me the power to overcome sin in my life?" We see here the difference between credence and dependence. We are not just cognitively depending on Christ, but we are surrendering volitionally to Him as well. You cannot have one without the other.

You could say, "Sure, I'll depend on and trust in Christ. He's a great guy and might make my life better." But there is no hope in such a philosophy. We cannot give this type of message to people who are suffering in the Middle East, or in the 10/40 Window, or in sub-Saharan Africa. Their lives will not be impacted by such a message. You can't just willingly say, "I'll trust Him" without knowing what you believe or even what you are saved from.

In the last chapter, we examined where every person stands in relationship with their Creator. We discussed how one can be forgiven of their sin and have an intimate relationship with God. And even though we covered a lot of detail, it may be helpful to talk about what salvation is NOT in order to solidify our understanding of salvation.

One technique to fully understand a concept is to examine the exact opposite. In looking at the contrast, we will gain a better understanding of the original concept. By studying the opposite idea, we have a more vivid understanding of what the verse is saying, so let's consider what true salvation is by examining what salvation is not.

WHAT SALVATION IS NOT...

1. The physical act of uttering words in prayer form

In Hebrews 4:2 we read, "...but the message they heard was of no value to them, because those who heard did not combine it with faith." Isn't that a sobering statement? The fact that the truth of God landed on ears, but it had no effect because it wasn't coupled with the heart of faith is a solemn thought, indeed. If you show a man a cue card and he spouts off, "I admit that I'm a sinner. I believe in my heart. I commit and accept Jesus Christ," I cannot automatically say to him, "You're saved!" Just getting someone to utter certain words is not evidence of salvation. The prayer of salvation must come from a heart that understands lost-ness, or as my friend Alvin Reid says, "their emptiness." They must understand they are lost before they can know the value of being saved.

You should be very cautious and patient when getting someone to utter a prayer of salvation because their heart must already know it and believe it. I am sad to say that I can recall a time in my high school days when my goal was to get someone to say "the prayer." I went to New York City as part of an evangelistic outreach, and I had been hearing about people who had great experiences leading people to Christ. I desired to have a great evangelism story too. So I determined in my heart that I would lead a person to the Lord that day. I remember sitting on a park bench when a gentleman approached. I can even picture his face. I remember trying to rush him to say "the prayer," and I remember telling him, "Just pray this and mean it in your heart." When I'd start to pray it, he'd interrupt me and say, "But you know, I don't know." Then I quickly answered, "Just say this prayer." I remember he finally got through the whole prayer, but I thought to myself, "I feel so bad because I just led him into the act of simply uttering words."

He walked away; I never saw him again and probably never will. I pray to God that He grips that man's heart and doesn't allow that scenario to skew his thinking about the gospel. You see, salvation is so much more than words. In fact, if an individual hears and recognizes the truth of the gospel and the state of their lostness, you can then explain to them how they can have an intimate relationship with God. You can explain the truth of Jesus Christ and how He is the God who came to earth, died for us and defeated death through His resurrection. You can share how the person needs to believe these cognitive facts, but also that person needs to volitionally trust Christ.

I believe the prayer is more of a confirmation or an affirmation for the mature believer to listen in to see if the one you are sharing the gospel with understands what they just did. Frankly, they could be saved before they ever utter that prayer. It's the heart that trusts. The mind cognitively knows, but it's the heart that trusts in the Savior. In Romans 10:9-10 we read, "That if you confess with your mouth, 'Jesus is Lord,' and believe in your heart that God raised him from the dead, you will be saved. For it is with your heart that you believe and are justified, and it is with your mouth that you confess and are saved." In the Jewish tradition, you could not say you were a believer without coupling it with action. It was absolutely, unequivocally, positively impossible to say "I'm a believer" and not live it in the 1st century Jewish custom. In Acts 2:38, when Peter says, "Repent and be baptized," we see that repentance is what literally brings salvation. The words expressing our faith in Christ are simply a confirmation of what has occurred inside us.

2. The physical act of walking down a church aisle during an invitation

Again, when people believe on Jesus Christ in their hearts during a church service, they are saved before they ever walk down the aisle. And maybe the prayer at the altar is a confirmation to believers who prayerfully watch as people come to Christ. As long as people cognitively believe and their hearts are stirred to salvation, they are probably saved prior to that physical act of walking down the aisle.

3. Contingent on a great emotion (or lack of) during the conversion experience

Some individuals, when they're leading a person to Christ, will gauge the success or effectiveness of this endeavor on the emotional reaction of that individual. This is not a good gauge at all. Emotion is based on personality and is no indication of spirituality or of whether or not salvation "took." Some cry and some laugh. I remember leading a man to the altar, explaining the truths of Christ, and praying with him as he received salvation. After praying at the altar he stood up, shook my hand and simply said, "That was the right thing to do. That was good that I did that." No tears. No emotion.

Conversely, some people who accept Christ bawl a river of tears and get very emotional, raising their hands and dancing all around. The way in which emotions are expressed will be reflected in the individuals' personalities. The Spirit may work mightily, but if the room is filled with introverts, they will be very introspective when they get moved by the truths of the songs and Scripture. You cannot gauge even your own worship on emotion and outward expression; it must be the heart stirring, and it may not always be an overt expression.

4. The result of solely wanting to be saved from going to hell upon death

"Do you want to go to heaven or hell?" I (Ben) am always curious if the person who asks this question expects to receive a different answer than "heaven." It seems to me this question may skew an unbeliever's answer and ignore the full teaching of salvation that we have been discussing in this chapter. Who would not choose heaven over hell? As a parent, I can't help but liken it to the question some parents often ask their child, "Do you want a spanking?" Think about what the child is going to say. Have you ever heard this response? "Yes! Actually, I'd like a double dose!"

Here's the problem, people don't understand the value of salvation until they understand their lostness. As we've discussed, because we are born in a sinful state, we have merited or earned condemnation to hell. It's not God being mean to us; it's our natural state. Because of Adam and Eve's choice, we've done it to ourselves. When a student of mine fails a course, I will say, "I did not fail you. You failed yourself by what you did or didn't do, and you are reaping the consequences of your actions." Likewise, because of mankind's sin nature – because I'm not perfect like God, and I'm not as holy as He is – there is no way I am worthy of heaven without God in me. I'm not holy and my sinful heart is repulsive to God and condemns me. I deserve eternal punishment for my sinful state. Therefore, I (and all sinners) need a change of heart—one that is life-changing and soul-changing. Every human being needs salvation through Christ.

The topic of hell should never be avoided because it is the inevitable outcome for those who do not accept Christ after they have been presented with the following truths:

– They are not at peace with God.

– They are in close relationship with God's wrath (Ephesians 2:3).

– They do not accept Christ's payment as the only way to appease the Father's wrath.

But hear me, I personally am of the conviction that if I turn to someone and ask, "Do you want to go to heaven or hell," they may not at that point fully understand their emptiness, or the fact that they are an enemy of God.

So I suggest that hell should definitely be part of the salvation equation, but we need to be aware that people who pray for salvation may not be thinking at the time, "I am not going to be punished eternally." The reason we are not saved is because we are not at peace with the Holy God, our Creator. As I said earlier, our Creator is the Holy One, and we must commit our lives to Him and ask forgiveness for how we have separated ourselves from Him and created a gulf between us through sin. And hell is a byproduct of the repercussion for not believing.

5. Translated into instant perfection

As stated in the previous chapter, the Bible disperses the full teaching of a particular doctrine within a number of related verses. But there are three terms that can summarize the different aspects of the salvation process.

Occasionally when the Scriptures use and refer to the word saved or salvation, it is actually used in a few different ways. It is used sometimes amorally – like you're saved from a ship sinking or you're saved from a crowd wanting to stone an individual. Literally, salvation is used in the sense of just protection. The word salvation was not a spiritual term that biblical writers made up; it was a very practical term that was adopted to explain the saving of our souls. Hence, the word saved has taken on this real spiritual meaning and it has great depth. So when we read Scripture sometimes when it uses the word saved it means the point in which you were justified, sanctified, or glorified. Let me explain.

JUSTIFICATION – SAVED FROM THE PENALTY OF SIN

The moment an individual is saved from the penalty of sin, we literally move from darkness to light, change course from hell to heaven, and gain peace with God. Sometimes the Bible uses the words saved or salvation to refer to the moment Christ redeems us. At the moment of salvation, the individual is sealed by the Holy Spirit and becomes a child of God – a Christian. This is called justification. In fact, Paul uses this word in Romans to describe that moment – it is a judicial act or a declaration wherein God proclaims, "You are justified!" It's as if a judge slams down the gavel and authoritatively states, "Done deal!"

SANCTIFICATION – SAVED FROM THE POWER OF SIN

Sometimes in Scripture, the word saved is referring to our developmental growth, spiritual growth, or maturity. Philippians 2:12 says, "Work out your own salvation." This is not referring to the justification aspect of salvation because you can't work out your own salvation. But you can work for, develop, and be in process of your spiritual maturity. And that's exactly what one of the terms for salvation refers to – sanctification. Once we are saved, we are to utilize the power of the Holy Spirit against the power of sin. The more you are sanctified, the more you are maturing, the more power you have against sinning because of the power source of the Holy Spirit within you. You have a mind that has been inculcated by His truths. You are to be constantly storing away and hiding God's Word in your heart. It is a lamp for your feet and a light for your path (Psalm 119:105). As you mature, you have the ability by God's power alone to say, "I'm not going to go down those old paths of sin again."

Before our salvation, according to Ephesians 2:1-3, we could not say "no" to sin. We could say, "I don't like doing these things," but we had no power to overcome the grip of sin. We, as sinners, were encased by sin. There was no way to jump out of that realm into the realm of the Holy Spirit. Now that we're in the saved realm, the Holy Spirit allows us to confidently state, "I don't want to do that action." We've been saved from the penalty of sin, and we gain an immediate power source that is our strength to overcoming the sins that once plagued our lives. We can be controlled by the Spirit (Ephesians 5:18) and therefore do not have to give in to the desires of our flesh.

GLORIFICATION – SAVED FROM THE PRESENCE OF SIN

Sometimes the word salvation will refer to the consummation of our salvation. In fact, Scripture writers will use the word saved to refer to our future salvation. The fact that the "helmet of salvation" (Ephesians 6:10-17) is looking at the future aspect of salvation means that one day we, as Christians, will be saved from this world and from this environment of sin. As Christians, our salvation is settled – a done deal. But one day we will be saved from the presence of sin when we see God face to face. There will be no more warring of the soul (Romans 7), and sin won't even be a variable in our lives. That's a beautiful place – to think that someday we won't have this battle within us! We will be in the presence of the Holy One for all eternity.

Recently, I (Ben) was lecturing on the benefits of heaven. I noted that we will be able to think, remember, worship, learn, work, and enjoy it all. You and I will be on the other side and we'll say, "Hey let's go worship the Holy One for a millennia or two!" And we'll just zip into His presence. There will be no sun because the glory of God illuminates the sky. We'll also recognize people and be able to talk to them, and we'll know who our loved ones are by name. What a beautiful hope we have as believers!

Titus 2:11-13 tells us, "For the grace of God that brings salvation has appeared to all men [justification]. It teaches us to say 'No' to ungodliness and worldly passions, and to live self-controlled, upright and godly lives in this present age [sanctification], while we wait for the blessed hope – the glorious appearing of our great God and Savior, Jesus Christ [glorification].

All three of these salvific terms are implied in that one passage. These terms are important to know because we evangelize to bring someone to God in order to be justified. We see that there is an accountability, or a discipleship process, that we must be involved in all the way through sanctification to glorification – it never ends. Salvation is a glorious promise and a wonderful gift of God.

"AM I SAVED?"

Now that we have taken some time to learn about what salvation is and what salvation is not, it's appropriate to ask yourself the most important question that you will ever be asked. Ask yourself, "Am I saved?"

We have covered a lot of ground in terms of the salvation experience and our desperate need for God because of our sin. But now it is time to ask if you are indeed a child of God. You may have been in church for a long time and heard many of these principles articulated in the pulpit. But as we've noted, salvation is more than simply hearing the message. If you examine your life, can you remember a time that you knelt before God and said, "I am a sinner and I need You to save me."? Maybe there has never been a time that you processed these things and cognitively looked at what you needed to know and believe in your heart to be saved. You didn't quite comprehend your lostness, so you haven't committed your heart and trusted Christ solely for salvation. I don't know where you are spiritually. Maybe you've lived in a Christian home and have possibly lived off your parents' belief system.

If there's never been a time where you have processed these things until now, please ask yourself, "Do I acknowledge this? Do I cognitively know this? Do I believe this in my heart? Have I volitionally, of my own will, committed and trusted in Jesus alone? Am I totally dependent on Him?"

Be cautioned. You can be right in the middle of the church house and be lost! You can be like Judas Iscariot who walked with Jesus for over three years, but he was lost. You can be like the Apostle Paul who, prior to his salvation experience, knew the Scripture writings but was looking at it through carnal eyes – as a works-based faith. He was essentially saying, "What can I do to get saved?" When he actually got saved, he was able to immediately become a strong minister because he knew all the truth from before, but now he was able to look at that same truth through spiritual eyes – Christ's eyes. You may know the Scriptures and all the spiritual words that so many Christians utter, but you may have learned after reading this chapter that you need to look at it differently now.

The question is this: If right now, you are not sure that you're saved (as defined in this chapter, based on God's Holy Word), would you like to take care of it now – in this moment? Would you bow your head and get in whatever posture that would cause you to focus on God and ask Him to forgive you and save you today?

WHAT MUST I DO?

In your heart you must (1) believe that Jesus is God; that He visited this earth, lived a sinless and pure life, died on the cross to make payment for your sin, arose from the tomb, and invites everyone to believe in Him; (2) believe that He arose the third day to give unequivocal proof that He is sufficient to conquer death, and He will conquer the spiritual death in our lives; (3) believe your soul will be eternally His if you know those facts, you couple that knowledge with a heart of faith, and put your dependence and trust in Him; (4) commit these things to Him by saying, "I believe You, and I will entrust my whole life to You based on this truth. My foundation will now be grounded on the truths of Jesus Christ, the Holy One of God."

Finally, in your own way, ask Jesus to be your Savior. And then, simply just thank Him for saving you, and thank Him that He has opened your eyes to your need of salvation.

If you have done this, God has washed and cleansed you, and your soul is as white as snow! God will give you a power source to say no to your temptations and to live for Him. You are beginning today as a Christian, as a child of God!

If you accepted Christ just now, we pray that you will inform someone of your decision, or contact either of us directly at Liberty University. We would love to rejoice with you. We pray that you will get involved in a church that teaches these principles from God's Word.

CHAPTER EIGHT

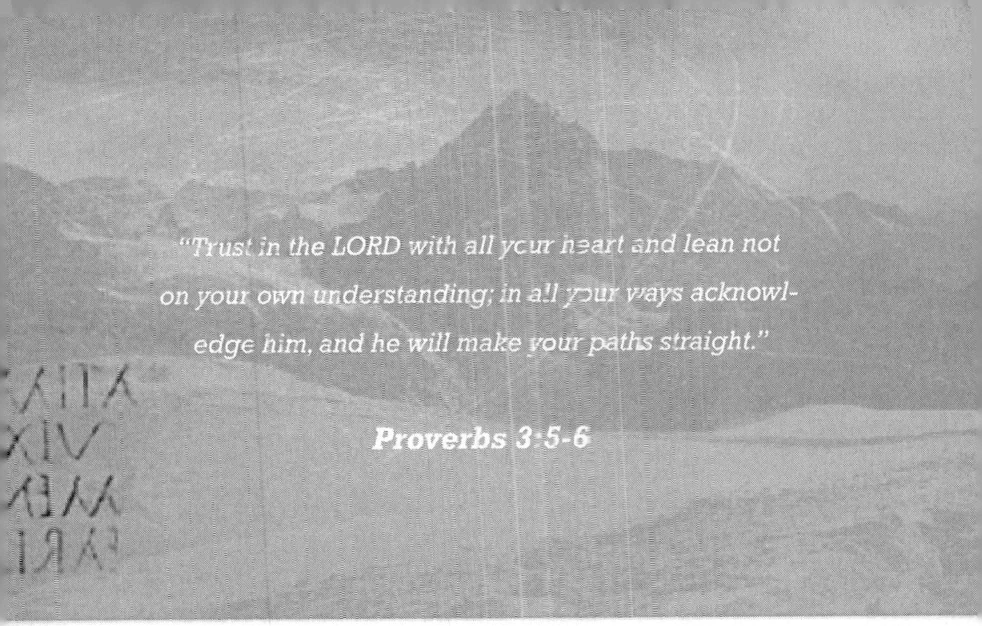
"Trust in the LORD with all your heart and lean not
on your own understanding; in all your ways acknowledge him, and he will make your paths straight."
Proverbs 3:5-6

APPROACHES TO MORAL DECISION-MAKING

EASIER SAID THAN DONE

A person's worldview should impact every area of their life including their decisions about right and wrong, and about good and evil. If a person adheres to a religious worldview, their religious texts, creeds, and the moral basis of their faith should have an influence on the way they behave when they are alone as well as in public. Unfortunately, no one is perfect in the application of their worldview. Everyone struggles at times to live the way they should, based upon their core beliefs. The Apostle Paul struggled with this as well when he said, "I know that nothing good lives in me, that is, in my sinful nature. For I have the desire to do what is good, but I cannot carry it out. For what I do is not the good I want to do; no, the evil I do not want to do - this I keep on doing." (Romans 7:18-19).

But what if one does not accept religious texts as an absolute guide for morality? Can a person be moral apart from God or from following a religious belief system? As human beings we are concerned about moral choices and their potential impact upon ourselves and those around us. Cultures establish moral laws which guide their citizens to make culturally acceptable choices for the collective good. Upon what foundation are those choices made? And who has the right to determine what is morally acceptable? Who has the right to legislate morality?

Historically there have been many approaches suggested to provide a guide to making moral decisions apart from God and the Bible, the Torah, the Qur'an or other religious texts. Although entire books have been written about these philosophical ideas we intend to only provide a basic introduction, synopsis, and a brief critique of these approaches to morality.

We would like to make one suggestion before we address these approaches to morality. If you approach moral decision-making from a Biblical/Christian worldview or other religious basis, we want to caution you to avoid syncretism. Syncretism, in context with worldviews, is the blending and unifying of ideas and concepts from different or opposing worldviews. As an example, if you come from a Biblical/Christian worldview, you should avoid integrating these secular moral philosophies into your lifestyle. Culture can have a great impact on the way you think and act. Consider how these moral philosophies may have infiltrated your own thinking and actions. How have these ideas affected the way that you practice your faith? Have they caused you in some ways to deny the God in which you placed your faith?

RELATIVISM

Relativism is the view that right and wrong are relative to one's culture, social group, or personal perspective. No moral absolutes exist. A moral absolute is a standard of right and wrong that is true at all times and in all places. It is not subject to change based upon individual or cultural perspectives. For example, from a Biblical/Christian worldview "You shall not murder" (Exodus 20:13) is a moral absolute. (It should be noted that murder is different from other forms of killing such as self-defense, military actions, and capital punishment). The morality of murder is not dependent upon a person's individual perspective or a culture's laws. From a Biblical/Christian worldview, it is wrong to commit murder, period. Relativism, however, would not adhere to the moral absolute that it is wrong to commit murder because whether or not something is right or wrong is all relative. In fact, historically, there are three different categories within the worldview of relativism.

The three prominent approaches to moral decision-making guided by the concept of relativism include, Cultural Relativism, Conventional Relativism and Subjective Relativism.

CULTURAL RELATIVISM

Cultural Relativism should be viewed from an anthropological perspective. This approach views things the way that they are, as opposed to the way they ought to be. It is assumed that what naturally occurs within cultures is the way things are supposed to occur. In her article, Anthropology and the Abnormal, Ruth Benedict (1887-1948), the famous anthropologist said, "We recognize that morality differs in every society and is a convenient term for socially approved habits. Mankind has always preferred to say, 'it is morally good' rather than, 'it is habitual'... but historically the two phrases are synonymous." From this perspective, morality is decided by culture. It is dependent upon culture and not on an external absolute standard. Cultural Relativism is a culturally autonomous approach to moral decision-making. Cultures decide for themselves what is morally good or bad by their laws and customs. Cultural tolerance is championed as a virtue and individual morality should be dependent upon cultural conditioning.

The fact of diversity between the morals of cultures is undeniable. Not only is there diversity between the moralities of nations, but diversity exists even between subcultures within nations. What is right and wrong is often conditioned by cultural traditions and laws. If a person is constantly told that an act is wrong, over time they may accept the idea as truth, even though they may act in opposition to their personally held belief. Just because this is what naturally happens within culture, should it be considered the basis for morality? Should morality be determined by one's culture? What are the potential problems with holding such a position?

First, the disagreement between cultures does not eliminate objective truth. If an act is immoral, it shouldn't be dependent upon the culture to recognize it as such. Secondly, Cultural Relativism commits the Naturalistic Fallacy. The Naturalistic Fallacy, remember, is making a conclusion about the way things ought to be based upon the way things are (or are assumed to be) within any particular setting. Just because a particular moral action naturally occurs within a culture does not necessarily make that action morally correct. If that were the case, any moral actions committed by a culture could be morally justified including the Nazi Holocaust. Countries that commit genocide, support human trafficking, train and use suicide bombers, abuse women, etc. would be morally justified if that is the way their culture practices their morality. Although anthropologists are more interested in reporting what is observed rather than stating a moral course for a culture, Cultural Relativism as an approach to moral decision-making has influenced and has helped shape cultural ideas.

CONVENTIONAL RELATIVISM

Conventional Relativism is similar to Cultural Relativism since it assumes the social and cultural nature of morality. Morality is determined by the culture in which one resides. Morality is dependent upon social acceptance. What is viewed as morally right in one culture may be viewed as morally wrong in another. In addition, individual morality is rejected. An individual then lives in harmony with society only as he or she submits his or her will to cultural norms.

Since morality is dependent upon culture, Conventional Relativism assumes that morals can be changed based upon the views of the culture. How does this occur? It occurs by the will or the vote of the majority. The will of the majority decides the morality for the whole.

How should one critique this view? Some would argue that an act is right or wrong because a referendum was brought before the people and a decision was made to establish a law. But if socially approved morality is always right and should be followed, then why should change ever take place? Why would the will of the people change to create new laws? The will of the people shouldn't change, but it does in fact occur.

From this viewpoint, those in the minority can and should be discriminated against since the majority makes the rules. If the majority of people believe that euthanasia of the elderly is necessary to curb health care costs, etc., then the elderly who are in the minority should support the decision and willingly die for the betterment of society.

Societies, like individuals, do not always know what is right or best for itself or their culture. Consider American history. Could the civil rights movement teach us anything about this approach to morality? Was America right in its discrimination against blacks and people of color? Is it morally right to kill millions of unborn children each year because they are a minority and cannot vote to protect themselves? Is it wrong to criticize the atrocities occurring in other countries against their own people because the majority believes it is fair and just? We believe it is illogical and immoral to think in such a way.

SUBJECTIVE RELATIVISM

Protagoras, the Greek philosopher and most famous of the Sophists is best known for his dictum, "Man is the measure of all things." Subjective Relativism is the approach to moral decision-making that makes the individual supreme. In 1739, David Hume, the Scottish philosopher said In A Treatise of Human Nature, "You can never find it (vice or fault) till you turn your reflection into your own breast, and find a sentiment of disapprobation (disapproval), which arises in you, towards this action." Hume was saying that what is right and wrong is determined by the individual and not by society.

Morality then is a matter of personal opinion. If you feel good after doing something, it is right for you. If you feel bad after doing something, it is wrong for you. Everyone has a right to her or his opinion, thus all opinions are right. Since there is no absolute agreement about what is right and wrong, there is no correct answer to moral disagreement. So what is the problem with this view? It creates moral confusion.

Like Cultural and Conventional Relativism, Subjective Relativism assumes there are no moral absolutes. However, when a person declares there are no absolutes they have just articulated an absolute statement of morality. Think about it. To say, "there are no absolutes" is an absolute.

In addition, two opposing views cannot both be right in the same context and in the same way. That would be a violation of the Law of Non-Contradiction. For example, two individuals cannot witness the act of stealing and one walk away believing it was morally correct and the other believe it was morally wrong. They both cannot be logically correct in their opposing views.

If you do not accept Subjective Relativism as truth, then as soon as a subjectivist tries to get you to believe their position, they have contradicted their position. If right and wrong is determined by the individual, then a subjectivist must hold his or her belief themselves without sharing that belief with others who disagree with them, or they have denied their own position.

It should be noted that people generally want to live by a subjective morality, but they want to be treated according to an objective morality. People want to live a guilt-free lifestyle and do what they please. "Live and let live" is their philosophy of life. But what if someone were to act in a selfish way to the detriment of the subjectivist? The subjectivist tends to demand an objective standard of morality to judge the offender. They want justice. Again, they have ultimately denied their own position.

TELEOLOGICAL APPROACHES

All teleological theories focus upon the results/ends of an act to determine the morality of that act. They differ as to which results are to be sought. These approaches are different from Deontological ones. A Deontological approach to moral decision-making is concerned about the means as well as the end results of an act. It is a duty-centered approach. Choices are made based upon moral rules and duties which are not to be violated.

In this section we will address four prominent teleological approaches. We will first look at Sensual Hedonism which focuses on the result that will bring about one's greatest personal pleasure and least amount of pain. The second approach is Rational Hedonism which can also be described as Egoism. This view focuses on the result that will be best for the individual in the long run. The third approach is Utilitarianism which is concerned about what is best for society as a whole. Lastly, we will consider Situationism or Joseph Fletcher's view of Situational Ethics. This view considers an act of love to be the end result one should seek when making a decision.

A general critique of teleological approaches finds some obvious concerns. First, most commit the naturalist fallacy. This will be clearly evident as each position is summarized. Secondly, apart from God, there is no final authority for establishing, requiring, or enforcing the theory. Most teleological approaches are naturalistic (Situationism excluded), and thus provide no basis for ultimate moral authority. Thirdly, since no human knows the future, no one can determine the action that will bring about the greatest possible results in the long run. Have you ever thought you were making a good choice and discovered later that you made a poor choice? Most would agree with this conclusion. So, if that is the case these approaches to moral decision-making are at best selfish, and at worst, morally detrimental to individuals and cultures.

SENSUAL HEDONISM

Sensual gratification should be the result of all actions. According to this approach, an act is right if, and only if, it maximizes one's pleasure and minimizes one's pain. Epicurus, the Greek Philosopher, has been falsely accused of supporting the idea of Sensual Hedonism. In his Letter to Menoeceus, Epicurus said, "For we recognize pleasure as the first good innate in us, and from pleasure we begin every act of choice and avoidance . . . using the feeling as the standard by which we judge every good." He was merely addressing what is clearly observable in humanity like an anthropologist. Humans want what feels good. "If it feels good then do it."

Humans are often more concerned about their pleasure than in doing what is right. For example, has someone ever broken their word to you only because a better option presented itself? They acted in a way that provided the greatest amount of pleasure for them without considering your feelings. Have you ever done that to someone else?

One of the problems with this approach to morality is the Hedonistic Paradox. It is the idea that the surest way to miss pleasure in life is to seek it as an end in itself. Solomon, the son of King David, experienced and shared this paradox. He attempted to find pleasure by seeking and amassing things he assumed would bring him pleasure. He declared in Ecclesiastes 2:10-11, "I denied myself nothing my eyes desired; I refused my heart no pleasure. My heart took delight in all my work, and this was the reward for all my labor. Yet when I surveyed all that my hands had done and what I had toiled to achieve, everything was meaningless, a chasing after the wind; nothing was gained under the sun." Even Solomon with his great wisdom fell prey to hedonistic ideas that produced nothing of value in his life.

RATIONAL HEDONISM (EGOISM)

Egoism is the idea that self-interest or personal happiness should be the goal of all actions. Since humans are naturally selfish (i.e. always act selfishly), it follows that an act is right if, and only if, it is done to benefit the one acting. Selfishness is perceived to be a virtue.

Ayn Rand, the noted American philosopher, supported this approach to moral decision-making. In 1962, she wrote in The Objectivist Newsletter, "Man — every man — is an end in himself, not the means to the ends of others. He must exist for his own sake, neither sacrificing himself to others nor sacrificing others to himself. The pursuit of his own rational self-interest and of his own happiness is the highest moral purpose of his life."

There are many problems with this approach to moral decision-making. First, the premise is impossible to prove. How can one say that all humans always act selfishly? Although it can be argued that some humans have sacrificed themselves for notoriety or selfish reasons, it cannot be shown that all humans act accordingly. Secondly, it robs relationships of the warmth and love that make them meaningful by making every act one for personal gain. It would assume that no one truly cares for others in a selfless way.

Thirdly, it commits the either/or fallacy. It falsely assumes that moral choices involve either exclusively caring for oneself, or exclusively caring for others at the expense of oneself. Finally, suffering purely for the benefit of others can be virtuous as well. Jesus Christ exemplified this when He suffered and died upon the cross for mankind's sin. "For Christ died for sins once for all, the righteous for the unrighteous, to bring you to God. He was put to death in the body but made alive by the Spirit" (1 Peter 3:18). Christ suffered and died not for His own benefit but for the benefit of the entire human race. Disciples of Christ are to follow His example of selflessness in word and deed. 1 John 2:6 states, "Whoever claims to live in him must walk as Jesus did."

UTILITARIANISM

Utilitarianism is the idea that the common good for all should be the goal of all actions. Since humans are social beings by nature, it follows that selfishness is not right. An act is right if, and only if, it results in the greatest happiness/ benefit/good for the greatest number of people. Jeremy Bentham and John Stuart Mill, his disciple, promoted and taught this concept of utility. Jeremy Bentham said in his, An Introduction to the Principle of Morals and Legislation, "Nature has placed mankind under two sovereign masters, pain and pleasure. It is for them alone to point out what we ought to do...." However this was not to be viewed as Egoism or selfishness. On the contrary, an individual was responsible to place his or her interests in harmony with the interests of the whole. He was concerned with what will bring about the greatest amount of pleasure or happiness to the greatest number of people.

John Stuart Mill in his famous work, Utilitarianism, stated that "Actions are right in proportion as they promote happiness, wrong as they tend to produce the reverse of happiness. By happiness is intended pleasure and the absence of pain; by unhappiness, pain and the privation of pleasure." Mill taught that the principle of utility was not about individual benefit but for the benefit of all concerned.

This sounds like a reasonable approach to morality. But should it be the basis for decision-making? Since happiness and pleasure are defined differently by people, whose definition of happiness and pleasure should be used? It is also impossible to calculate whether or not the majority of people are truly happy and better off because of individual or government decisions. It has also historically led to many injustices and violations of human rights for the sake of the "common good."

The principle of utility is often used by the government to make decisions that are intended to benefit the majority of its citizens. For example, parole, setting a criminal free early based upon good behavior, is an example of utilitarianism in action. It can be illustrated with the great debate about the problem of overcrowded prisons. New prisons could be built to accommodate the overcrowding, but then taxes would have to be raised to build the prisons. If more prisoners are housed, then more staff and security must be hired. The taxpayer is responsible to feed, clothe and provide health care to these prisoners. The masses are taxed and impacted by this decision. However, to avoid this mass discomfort, prisoners who may not be rehabilitated are released on parole. They may commit a criminal act again but the crime only impacts a few individuals instead of the whole of society. Thus, in utilitarianism, the negative impact of releasing a prisoner early is better than the negative impact on an entire community or state.

SITUATIONISM/SITUATIONAL ETHICS

The basic concept behind Situational Ethics is that the most loving thing should be the goal of all actions in any given situation. Who can argue with that concept? The questions that must be answered are: "What is the meaning of love?" "What type of love should be sought after and practiced?" "And whose definition of love should be used?"

Joseph Fletcher wrote his famous work, Situation Ethics: The New Morality in 1966. In the 60's he witnessed the turmoil of moral issues and viewed his moral approach to decision-making, Situationism, as the balance between legalism and antinomianism (lawlessness). Legalism was oppressive and unacceptable. It was based upon rules and regulations. Antinomianism was the view that right and wrong was decided in the situation without any specific moral principles to guide it. By championing love as the basis for morality, Fletcher was attempting to provide a Christian approach to morality that could be accommodating to a variety of cultural perspectives.

According to Fletcher, love is the highest good, therefore an act is right if and only if it reflects the most loving thing you can do in any situation—even if it means breaking traditional moral rules (like the Ten Commandments) to do it. In his chapter "Love Is Not Liking," Fletcher provided an example of doing the loving thing even if it meant violating biblical morality to do so. He states, "A young unmarried couple might decide, if they make their decisions Christianly, to have intercourse (e.g., by getting pregnant to force a selfish parent to relent his over-bearing resistance to their marriage). But as Christians they would never merely say, 'It's alright if we like each other!' Loving concern can make it all right, but mere liking cannot" (Fletcher, p. 104).

"The ruling norm of Christian decision is love: nothing else" (Fletcher, p. 69). According to Joseph Fletcher, love trumps law. But there are many potential problems with this view of morality. First, to say that love supersedes all other commandments is a gross misinterpretation of Scripture (Romans 13:8-10) Love fulfills, it does not annul, the law. Love and law are not mutually exclusive ideas. The law shows us how to apply love.

When the Pharisees asked Jesus a question regarding the greatest commandment, "Jesus replied: 'Love the Lord your God with all your heart and with all your soul and with all your mind.' This is the first and greatest commandment. And the second is like it: 'Love your neighbor as yourself'" (Matthew 22:37-39). He also said, "If you love Me, keep My commandments" (John 14:15). Love and Law are compatible and not legalistic in nature.

Another problem with this view is that it ignores the possibility that

God's commands may be given for our benefit, and are thus a product of His wisdom and love for us. Moses, speaking to the children of Israel, said in Deuteronomy 10:12-13, "And now, Israel, what does the LORD your God require of you, but to fear the LORD your God, to walk in all His ways and to love Him, to serve the LORD your God with all your heart and with all your soul, and to keep the commandments of the LORD and His statutes which I command you today for your good?" Here God's commands are not to harm or hinder His people, but they were intended for their benefit.

Finally, like all teleological theories, Situational Ethics mistakenly assumes that you can either know or calculate what will be the best for all of the parties involved. In any given situation, how can humans, who are finite beings, choose the most loving thing to do apart from God's revelation? How can they ultimately know the end result of their decisions? It is once again impossible to determine.

WHO WILL YOU TRUST?

So how do you personally make decisions about right and wrong? What approach do you use in various circumstances to guide you in making a decision? If you approach morality from a Biblical/Christian worldview, do you consistently use the Bible to direct your thoughts about morality, or have these other philosophical approaches influenced your thinking? We mentioned avoiding syncretism at the beginning of this chapter. Like the children of Israel who followed and believed in God but also worshiped and formed images to Baal, do you believe in God but in practice do you follow the world and its approach to morality?

It is our prayer that God's Word, the Bible, will be your guide to making moral decisions. And when you don't know what to do, you will seek the truths found in His Word and rely upon the leading of the Lord to light your path. "Trust in the LORD with all your heart and lean not on your own understanding; in all your ways acknowledge him, and he will make your paths straight" (Proverbs 3:5-6).

We look forward to sharing more about how you can personally apply what you are learning in these chapters. We will continue to give guidance about how to fulfill the will of God for your life. And throughout the remainder of the book, we will discuss further how to mature spiritually.

CHAPTER **NINE**

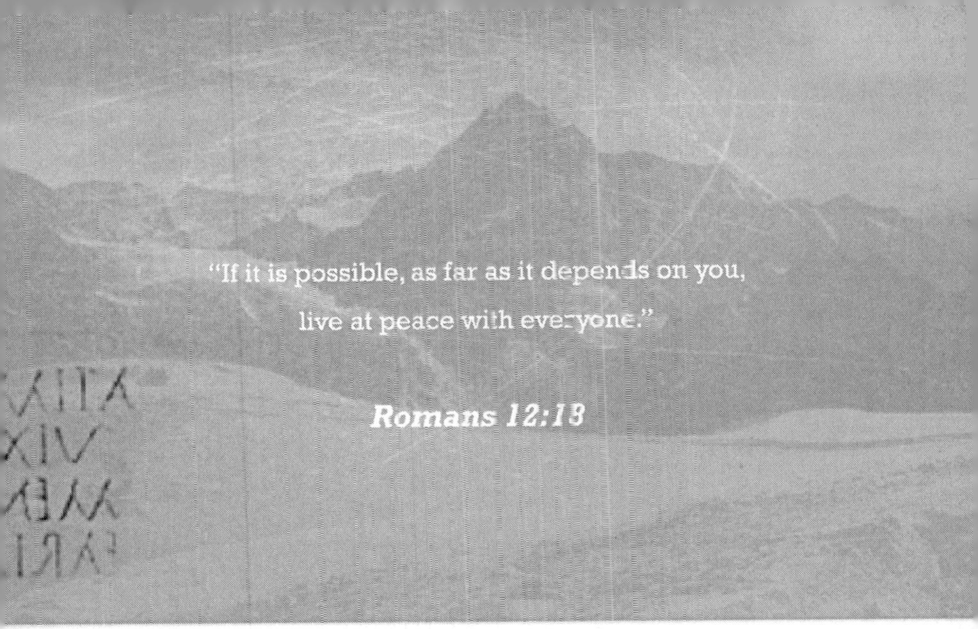
"If it is possible, as far as it depends on you,
live at peace with everyone."
Romans 12:18

TRUE TOLERANCE

When you hear the word "tolerance" what comes to mind? What words, ideas or visions pop up as you think about the question, "Are people tolerant today?" When asking students these questions another word surfaces, "intolerant." It is often perceived in our world today that people are intolerant of each other. Frequently the question is asked, "Why can't people just get along?" That's a very good question. But the answer might surprise you. It is because we no longer understand what it means to be tolerant.

Words have a way of changing their meaning over time. For example, the word charity in the King James Version of the Bible was used to describe how Christians should love one another. (1 Corinthians 13:1-8a). It is a translation of the Greek word, "agape" which can be interpreted to mean "unconditional love." However, when you hear the word charity used today it is interpreted to mean benevolence. It is the idea of providing food, money, time or other essentials to a worthy cause. Similarly, the same is true about the word tolerance. Although by definition the word has not changed, its meaning has dramatically changed in our culture.

TOLERANCE DEFINED

According to Webster's New World Dictionary, the word tolerate means "to allow," "to respect (others' beliefs, practices, etc.) without sharing them," and "to bear or put up with (someone or something disliked)." If one were to follow this definition of tolerance, how would this look in everyday life regarding one's beliefs?

Let's dissect this definition a little more closely. A person is tolerant when they "allow" another person to have a different opinion than their own. In chapter two we discussed the nature of opinions. Everyone should have the right to their own opinion. However, having a right to an opinion does not make every opinion right, including your own. By definition, when you do not allow another person the right to have an opinion different than your own, you are not being tolerant towards that person.

Have you ever heard some say to you, "You're too opinionated."? What do they mean by that statement? They might mean that you share your ideas as the only legitimate beliefs to have, and everyone else is wrong—you are too dogmatic about your beliefs. They might mean that every time a topic comes up for discussion you always have to add "your two cents worth" to the conversation rather than listening to others' opinions. Open-mindedness and acceptance of others' beliefs as true and valid is viewed as a higher virtue than personal beliefs and convictions. This is where the definition of tolerance goes astray.

A person is also tolerant when they "respect (others' beliefs, practices, etc.) without sharing them." The definition becomes a little more difficult to put into practice at this point. If you respect someone, you value and esteem them. In the context of opinions, you would value and appreciate their beliefs without sharing them. When you listen to them, you show them that they have value and that you care about their opinion. By the simple act of listening to others, you are expressing love. You can love someone and also disagree with them. That is why Jesus could tell His disciples, "But I tell you: Love your enemies and pray for those who persecute you." (Matthew 5:44).

How do you feel about a person when they share an opinion different from your own? Do you immediately want to "set them straight" and "correct" their false beliefs? Although this may be a natural reaction for some, it usually isn't the right approach. This attitude can sever relationships or build a wall between people. This type of response can also cause a Christian to lose the opportunity to share their faith with someone. Although they might be sincere in their beliefs, their approach is perceived as sincerely wrong.

It is important to remember that respecting other's beliefs does not mean that you have to agree with them. It also does not mean that you shouldn't want to influence them to change their beliefs if you believe they are wrong. However, the true definition of tolerance means that you respect the person enough to allow them to have a differing opinion. It means that you value them as a person, but you can engage them intellectually and lovingly regarding ideas and beliefs.

Finally, a person is tolerant when he/she is willing to "bear or put up with (someone or something disliked)." Have you ever had a conversation or several conversations with a person and you just can't come to an agreement? They have shared their beliefs and opinions, and you just couldn't accept them as truth. Likewise, you have shared your beliefs or opinions with them, and they didn't change their mind. Continuing to live, work and associate with them in a cordial way is true tolerance in action. In summary, tolerance should be viewed in reference to how we respond to the people we disagree with, not how we respond to the ideas we think are false.

Having different opinions, though, does not negate objective truth. The truth of the matter may not have been discovered by one or both of you, but truth should not be displaced by personal opinion. This concept, however, has been almost eradicated by postmodernism. Today, the terms truth and tolerance have taken on a whole new meaning.

TRUTH AND TOLERANCE IN CONTEMPORARY POSTMODERNISM

Although the term has been around for decades, Postmodernism as a cultural phenomenon has redefined the terms truth and tolerance. Josh McDowell and Bob Hostetler in their book The New Tolerance provide a good synopsis of Postmodernism and its impact on the term "truth" from the 1960's -1990's. In summary, there is no object truth. Absolute truth does not exist and every concept of truth is relative to one's culture. Since truth is created by the culture "individuality is an illusion" and any criticism of culture is unjustified.

Since the mid-nineties the concept of truth has become more subjective in nature. Its roots can be traced much earlier but the impact of Postmodernism continues to have its effect upon cultural and especially individual beliefs. Truth has become relative to an individual's perspective rather than a cultural one. Truth is assumed to be created by the individual. What is true to one person may not be necessarily true to someone else.

It can be stated this way, "I have my truth and you have your truth." This is perceived to be factual even when the two individuals are in disagreement about the same subject. If a person is confronted with someone else's concept of truth that seems truer than their concept of truth, they may accept the other person's truth as their own. But even then, "truth" is subject to change. It sounds confusing doesn't it? That is because it violates logic. In particular, it violates the Law of Non-Contradiction also known as the Law of Contradiction.

The Law of Non-Contradiction states that something cannot both exist and not exist or be true and false at the same time and in the same way. We touched on this law of logic in chapter 6. For example, either God exists or He doesn't exist. There is not a third option. Two people can be debating about the morality of Capital Punishment in relation to a person on death row. The statement is made, "It is morally right to take this person's life." One person believes that it is morally correct for the government to end the life of a mass murderer. They would agree that the statement is "true." The other person believes it is morally wrong to end the criminal's life. They would assert that the statement is "false." It violates the Law of Non-Contradiction for both of them to walk away from the debate believing that they are both right. They may do so, but it is not logically sound.

Truth is not something that is relative to a person's opinion. It is not based upon where a person grows up or their perception of reality. It is not based upon one's feelings or attitudes. Truth is not created, but it can be discovered regardless of one's current cultural understanding of the term.

All truth is God's truth. David declared in Psalm 31:5 "Into your hands I commit my spirit; redeem me, O LORD, the God of truth." Jesus Christ said, "I am the way and the truth and the life" (John14:6). God has given man the ability to think, create and to reason. However, man in his pride comes to the conclusion that he or she can establish truth apart from God. When mankind thinks this way, it is a fulfillment of the Apostle Paul's words in Romans 1:25 when he said, "They exchanged the truth of God for a lie, and worshiped and served created things rather than the Creator - who is forever praised. Amen."

Postmodernism has not only affected modern culture's understanding of truth but also the concept of tolerance. In today's re-defined concept, to be truly tolerant means that you must agree that another person's opinion is just as valid as your own. You must give your approval, your endorsement, and your sincere support to their beliefs and many times to their behaviors. In contrast to the traditional definition of tolerance, the new tolerance of today communicates the ideas that whatever a person believes is equally true and equally valid. And to say that someone is wrong is now considered to be intolerant. Gregory Koukl provides a clear example of this in his article, When Tolerance Is Intolerant (2003). He spoke to a group of seniors at a Christian high school in Des Moines, and he addressed the issue of tolerance. He began by writing two sentences on the board. He wrote:

> "All views have equal merit and none should be considered better than another."
> "Jesus is the Messiah and Judaism is wrong for rejecting that."

After completing the first sentence the students nodded to show their approval of the sentence. When he completed the second sentence, hands began to rise across the classroom. Students began sharing their disapproval of it by saying that to make such a statement was intolerant. They believed it violated the first statement. However, upon closer investigation of the statements the students came to realize that the second statement was an opinion supported by the first statement. It was the confusion caused by the new tolerance definition that made these statements appear to be contradictory. Koukl notes:

> If all views have equal merit, then the view that Christians have a better view on Jesus than Jews is just as true as the idea that Jews have a better view on Jesus than Christians. But this is hopelessly contradictory. If the first statement is what tolerance amounts to, then no one can be tolerant because "tolerance" turns out to be gibberish.

Do you see the dilemma? The problem with the new tolerance is that the only opinion that is acceptable is no opinion. When two differing opinions are held, someone is intolerant which is illogical. Tolerance should be practiced in relationship to how we treat people, not ideas we believe are false. The problem with the new tolerance is especially troubling in two areas: ethics and religion.

THE NEW TOLERANCE AND ETHICS: RELATIVISM

The new tolerance has disguised itself in a popular approach to moral decision-making called relativism. Ethical Relativism is the idea that right and wrong are dependent upon an individual or cultural perspective. Absolute truth statements regarding right and wrong do not exist. For example, a relativist would argue that you can hold a belief that is "true for you" as long as it does not conflict with what another person's right to believe what is "true for them." The same can be said about cultures. Although they reject the belief in absolutes, they have adopted their own absolutist belief called "tolerance." But a closer investigation into this idea of ethical tolerance reveals its shortcomings.

Anthropologists have come to the conclusion that since moral diversity exists around the world, then right and wrong must be dependent upon one's culture. Diversity is undeniable. But does the fact of diversity eliminate objective truth? We do not think so. For example, can the moral actions of an individual or a culture be criticized? We believe that they can be criticized. Individuals and societies do this all of the time and for good reason. Is it immoral for a person or a culture to say that Adolf Hitler and the Nazi Holocaust were wrong? Is it intolerant to say that a father is wrong if he tortures and kills his two-year-old daughter for pleasure? Is the practice of slavery by a landowner or a culture morally justified? These are extreme examples, but they are necessary to make a point. If right and wrong are dependent upon a culture or an individual, then criticism is unjustified.

It can be argued at this point, "These examples are erroneous because they hurt others." But who has the right to decide whether an act hurts another individual or a culture? It has been argued that abortion should remain legal because of a mother's right to choose. Her right to privacy gives her the right to end the life of a child growing within her womb. But doesn't abortion hurt and kill a baby? In a 7-2 vote, the United States Supreme Court ruled in Roe v. Wade that a child in the womb is not a person and is not protected by the Constitution. In essence, seven individuals eliminated state rights and gave women in the U.S. the legal right to an abortion.

The question is then asked, "Is abortion right or wrong?" How does one come to a conclusion? According to relativism; it depends. It depends upon an individual's conscience and/ or a culture's rules for right and wrong. But what if these views of relativism are in conflict? What if abortion wasn't an option, but was a mandate of the government? Relativism becomes intolerant to individual choice. The answer becomes the problem. In actuality, relativism is inconsistent logically and cannot be lived out in the real world. Ethical tolerance sounds like it is the answer to our moral dilemmas, but in actuality it is a moral dilemma itself.

THE NEW RELIGIOUS TOLERANCE: BAHA'I

Have you ever heard the phrases, "There are many paths to God," or "God is big enough for all religions." When you hear these types of statements it is assumed that they are the only acceptable ones to hold. Every other belief is intolerant. But are they logical? This type of religious tolerance is called Baha'i. Baha'i is the religious belief in the unity of God, religion and mankind. The followers of Baha'i are free to believe the religion of their choice as long as they accept the religious beliefs of all others. Exclusivity is rejected. All religious positions are viewed to be in unity with each other. But how is this possible?

Traditional tolerance would say that individuals have the right to believe any religious belief or none at all. But the new tolerance would recognize all beliefs as acceptable. As noted earlier, to believe that God exists as well as to believe that God does not exist is a violation of the Law of Non-Contradiction. One view is right and another view is wrong. That is not being intolerant, that is being logically sound. Let's argue for a moment that God does exist. The new tolerance would indicate that all religious views regarding God are equal and valid. But is such a position plausible? If so, God is a contradiction within Himself, and His communication with mankind does not make sense. Let's look at a summary of some major religious beliefs about God.

Hinduism – Diversity exists but God is Brahman, an eternal essence. When one's atman (indestructible soul or self) unites with Brahman, one is united as a part of God.

Buddhism – God may or may not exist. This was not a central theme of the teachings of the Buddha. God could have been the first cause, or "the big bang" could have been the cause of existence. The ultimate goal is not to know God but to achieve Nirvana which is a passionless state of existence.

Judaism – God is One. He is known by His attributes and is above His creation, including mankind. God is eternal and the supreme judge. His commandments in the Torah are to be followed as well as the teachings of His prophets in order to achieve salvation.

Islam – God is Allah. He is One and has no equal or partners. His final prophet to mankind is Muhammed and the Qur'an is to be strictly followed.

Christianity – God is viewed as one God in three Persons: Father, Son, and Holy Spirit.

If one were to accept each of the above views as equal and valid, then God is at best, contradictory and at worst, evil. How can God be One with no equal as well as be non-existent? How can God be the God of Abraham, Isaac and Jacob as well as Allah who has revealed the truth to his final prophet, Muhammed and the teachings of the Tanakh (Hebrew Bible) all be correct? How can God be a Trinity and the second Person of the Trinity, Jesus Christ teach that He was God (John 8:58) and that He was the only way to the Father (John 14:6)?

To believe there are many paths to God is to assume that God is the same. This idea is clearly false as has been illustrated. It also assumes the illogical, that God has revealed Himself in many different ways and forms, and we all end up where our religious faith takes us. This, as well, is nonsensical. Therefore, religious study should not be about accepting everyone's views, but about seeking the truth.

A CHRISTIAN RESPONSE TO TOLERANCE

Christians have often been labeled as intolerant. We are not concerned about the new concept of tolerance, but we want to focus on the traditional view. How well do Christians follow New Testament instruction about getting along with others and being tolerant? If you claim to be a Christian, how truly tolerant are you of other people with whom you disagree? In this final section we would like to look at five verses of Scripture to reveal the Apostle Paul's instructions to the Church at large about how they should treat others within the Church as well as outside of the Church. Each of these passages will be translated from the New International Version. Romans 12:16 – "Live in harmony with one another. Do not be proud, but be willing to associate with people of low position. Do not be conceited." The Bible often describes a relationship of unity among believers (John 17:23). Christians are to have a spirit of cooperation and acceptance. Pride is rebuked by God (James 4:6) because the proud are acting in the place of God. Christians are to value others better than themselves (Philippians 2:3). From this passage one can see that God expects the Church (Christians who claim to believe in Christ as their Savior) to get along with others because of the way they should view people and themselves.

Romans 12:18 – "If it is possible, as far as it depends on you, live at peace with everyone." How much clearer can Paul handle the issue of tolerating those with whom Christians disagree? Christians should be peaceable toward those who have a different opinion than themselves. "Everyone" would include both individuals who are Christians and those who are not Christians. Paul understands, though, that any conflict is a two-way street. So his advice is limited to the individual who claims to be a Christian. You cannot change how the other person responds. You can only decide how you will respond.

Ephesians 4:2 – "Be completely humble and gentle; be patient, bearing with one another in love." Humility and gentleness are seen as a virtue and not a sign of weakness. Unconditional love should be shown to all individuals. Paul addressed the issue of love in 1 Corinthians 13. In verse four, the first way love is described is "patient." Have you ever become impatient with a person who disagreed with you? Since God is love (1 John 4:16), when a Christian acts in patience toward someone, they are acting in the likeness of God. Here we see the phrase "bearing with one another in love." Does it remind you of the traditional definition of tolerance, to "bear or put up with (someone or something disliked) ?" However, the Bible adds the concept "in love." That is because only with God's help can a Christian live the life of tolerance while loving the person unconditionally.

Ephesians 4:32 – "Be kind and compassionate to one another, forgiving each other, just as in Christ God forgave you." Kindness and compassion are often missing in human relationships. But they are attributes of the Lord Jesus Christ and ones that Christians should exemplify toward others. It is when Christians see people the way the Lord sees them that they can truly begin to minister to one another. It is when people are viewed from God's perspective with value and potential that lives can be impacted for Christ. The Bible teaches that everyone is a sinner (Romans 3:23). When a Christian is hurt by someone else, how should they respond? Often, it is with shock, as if they were exempt from hurting others. God's Word challenges a Christian's traditional thinking by not requiring them to forgive the way other people forgive them, but how

God has forgiven them. The same idea is communicated in Colossians 3:13, "Bear with each other and forgive whatever grievances you may have against one another. Forgive as the Lord forgave you." That is immeasurable forgiveness. That is genuine love in action.

Galatians 6:10 – "Therefore, as we have opportunity, let us do good to all people, especially to those who belong to the family of believers." What opportunities are presented in Christians' lives to be good toward others? Love is an action verb. It is a decision and an act that can be performed to positively impact the lives of others. The Apostle John said, "By this all men will know that you are my disciples, if you love one another" (John 13:35). Take a moment to consider in what ways you have seen Christians show God's love to others? Can you think of some examples in your church, your home, or in your neighborhood? Have you personally experienced that kind of unconditional love in action—as the giver or as the receiver? How well do you love others?

In conclusion, traditional tolerance is the only concept of tolerance that actually can be practiced by individuals. It is a concept that needs to be shared and practiced by everyone, including Christians. It is the way the gospel of Jesus Christ should be shared with a skeptical world. It does not mean that people should not have the right to share their opinions, including religious ones. Christians should never capitulate to the idea that sharing one's faith is somehow morally or theologically wrong. That would be intolerant towards Christianity. Peter admonished Christians, "But in your hearts set apart Christ as Lord. Always be prepared to give an answer to everyone who asks you to give the reason for the hope that you have. But do this with gentleness and respect" (1 Peter 3:15). Paul told Timothy, "And the Lord's servant must not quarrel; instead, he must be kind to everyone, able to teach, not resentful. Those who oppose him he must gently instruct, in the hope that God will grant them repentance leading them to a knowledge of the truth, and that they will come to their senses and escape from the trap of the devil, who has taken them captive to do his will" (2 Timothy 2:24-26).

Every belief has an element of exclusivity. What you believe should not be based upon where you grew up or what you have been taught by others. What you believe should be based upon truth. That is a journey worth taking. That is a goal worth finding.

And if you haven't guessed yet... We believe that truth is found only in Jesus Christ. And we believe its time to share that life-changing truth with you now.

We trust that throughout these pages, we have earned a hearing with you so that you will consider the message of salvation that can only be found through Jesus Christ.

CHAPTER TEN

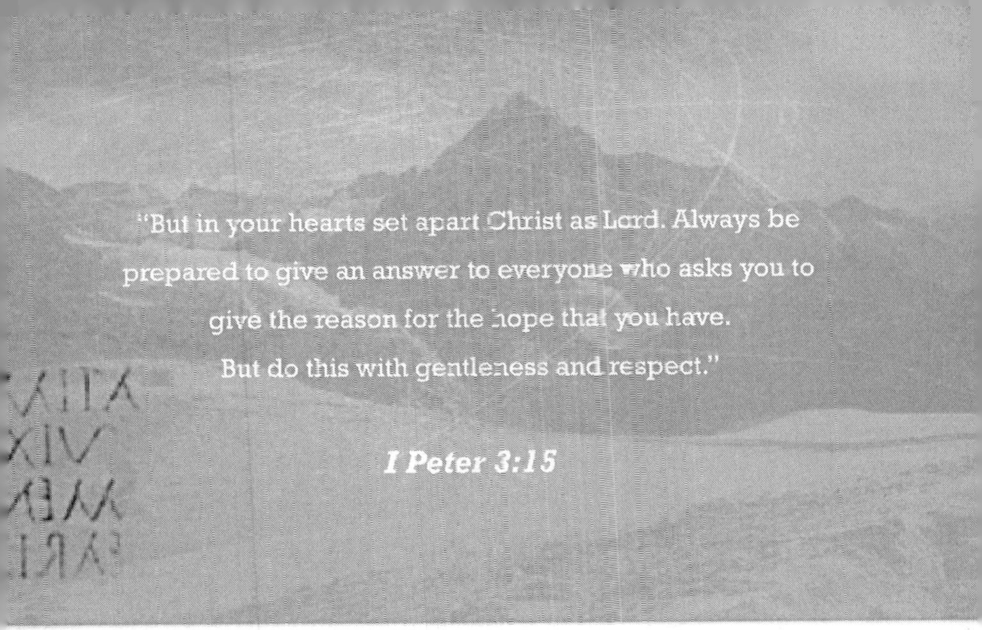

"But in your hearts set apart Christ as Lord. Always be prepared to give an answer to everyone who asks you to give the reason for the hope that you have. But do this with gentleness and respect."

I Peter 3:15

GIVE IT A TRY

SHARE WITH OTHERS

Nothing will instill a doctrine, life-lesson, principle, or skill into a person's mind more than having to teach it to someone else. Teaching forces a person not only to study a particular topic so they comprehend it, but also to study the material with the goal to present it clearly so others can understand it as well.

The same is true in the development of our spiritual lives. Spending time reading the Bible and other writings is indeed a great start, but a person can better instill in themselves biblical truths by also teaching or sharing these truths with others. This chapter will give you suggestions as to how you can practically share with others the same truths that you are currently learning.

The manner in which we present spiritual truth may vary depending on the audience. However, the message must remain the same. For instance, the way spiritual truth is presented to a child would be different from the way that same truth would be presented to an unsaved adult. Yet, we want to caution you in this regard. We must be careful never to compromise the truth for the sake of the audience. We cannot skew any fact of the gospel, or leave out any detail regardless of the individual, environment, or scenario.

With my (Ben's) biblical studies students, I encourage them to learn how to convert theological definitions into language a four-year-old could comprehend. One stipulation is that they cannot cut corners on the truth. I assign them a word like sanctification and give them fifteen minutes to discuss it amongst themselves. Then I ask them to demonstrate how they would explain the concept of sanctification to a four-year-old.

Another group is assigned the word heart. I tell them the heart is the center and seat of our emotions, the very decision force within us. The heart is the center of our will. Then I ask them to demonstrate how they would explain these ideas to a four-year-old. The mind of a child and their innocence is fascinating. A pastor once told me a story about a man in his congregation who had a heart transplant. When a child heard about the heart transplant, she asked the man if he needed to ask Jesus into his heart again. Of course we think that's sweet; we can picture a child saying that because they think in literal terms. Obviously, there's a deeper meaning. When we use the phrase, "ask Jesus into our heart," we are asking Him to infuse that decision into our heart, into the center and seat of our emotion and intellect, into our very being.

Unfortunately, I believe in our current society some are more interested in the presentation than with the truth of what is being presented. All throughout the Gospels, Jesus Himself was very cognizant of how He presented truth to individuals. He too seemed to feel that presentation was important. For example, in talking about giving alms, He brought up nuances about the theater. He says (paraphrased), "Your right hand shouldn't know what your left hand is doing, but you guys would rather parade around and blow trumpets as you give your alms"(Matthew 6:2-4). And that's a picture of the theater. Key actors would walk through the main road of the city to the theater, and they would applaud and blow trumpets. That was the way Jesus related to them. I think the presentation is very important. I am all about being creative. In fact, the more creative tools to attract the listener the better. However, the ultimate goal is to preach the unadulterated gospel message. so I just want to talk briefly about the manner in which we convey these truths. And I would like to do so by revisiting some familiar Bible verses that we referenced earlier in this book.

BE READY

The manner in which we present the truths of the biblical teaching of salvation is definitely addressed in Scripture, and it is very important to highlight these verses concerning how we should share the gospel. Please view these few verses as different tools in a tool belt. If you are anything like me (Ben), I call my father or friends to help me with odd jobs because I am not a handy man, by any means. These guys all have well-equipped tool belts. When they approach a certain job, they grab the right tool and get to work. They don't waste time running to the other side of the house to grab another tool. All of their tools are "on the ready." It would be a little ridiculous if we hired a handy man that only had one tool on his tool belt, and he used that one tool for every single job. Likewise, we want you to look at these different methods of sharing the gospel as different tools. There may be an occasion where you are more forceful, but then there may be times where you can simply converse with a person. Let's take a look at a few methods.

1 Peter 3:15 says, "But in your hearts set apart Christ as Lord. Always be prepared to give an answer . . . ." It's this word answer that is really interesting. There are many ways to give answers. You can respond militarily, competitively, angrily, or passively. In Scripture there are different ways to give an answer as well. In the book of Colossians, Paul answers back some opponents polemically,

which literally means to wage war. You can understand why he would do that because they claimed that Jesus Christ was not God. Rather, they said that Jesus was a nice angel – and He and every other angel must be worshiped – but they argued that Jesus was not really God; nor was He sufficient for salvation. So Paul is very polemic in Colossians 1:15-18 when he said, "He [Christ] is the image of the invisible God, the firstborn over all creation. For by him all things were created: things in heaven and on earth . . . And he is the head of the body, the church . . . ." Paul was very specific and very bold in his answer to the Colossians.

In 1 Peter 3:15 the word answer is the term that means to give an answer, but it is used in the sense as a lawyer would give an answer in a courtroom. A lawyer has to use a systematic approach and have a well thought-out argument when he presents his case (a detailed illustration regarding the preparation of a courtroom lawyer was described in Chapter 1).

Long gone is the response given in the Scopes trials, "God said it, I believe it, and that settles it." That answer branded Christians as being uneducated. If His Word is truth, it will be able to stand the test of any examination, successfully refuting any scrutiny – so it is fine to put it to the test. God's Word is much like an anvil. Many things are pounded upon it and tools may wear down, yet the anvil stands. That's the Word of God. So be systematic, be thoughtful, be well-prepared and be ready to give answers. Incidentally, we have observed that preparation breeds confidence. It is healthy to be well-prepared and ready to field arguments and questions, and it is wise to know what principles guide your answers.

REASON WITH THEM

Paul reasoned with them and asked people to reason with him. It's important to know that God is very aware of our life and our circumstances. In 1 Corinthians it says that Apollos watered and Paul preached, and they were considered to be equals in ministry. We all ought to share the gospel to bring a person to a decision, yet if they don't come to a decision immediately, ask them to consider these spiritual truths again. It's okay after you've sensed a hesitation to ask them to reason and think it over. You do not want to stir their emotions for the sole purpose of getting the response you're looking for. Take it from us, they may be emotionally stirred, but you do not want to stir their emotions just to hear them say the desired words. Rather, you want their heart to be changed. There are some individuals that need time to process all the truth you have just presented. Give the seed of truth time to take root.

HAVE RESTRAINT

Another passage that is often overlooked is 1 Corinthians 1:18. It talks about having restraint and not quickly being offended. "For the message of the cross is foolishness to those who are perishing, but to us who are being saved it is the power of God." In other words, when you talk to someone about the gospel, you have to approach the conversation with a level of restraint. Even though you know the precious truth and understand the glorious gospel, the most intelligent unbeliever cannot fully comprehend the preciousness of the gospel until the moment they are convicted to accept Christ. They can watch the movie The Passion and be stirred, but those who are unbelievers can never really know the precious treasure they are treading on. In Matthew 7:6 it says, "Do not ... throw your pearls to pigs. If you do, they may trample them under their feet..." Literally, it is this precious jewel these animals do not even understand. They are pushing the pearls around with their noses and stomping on them with their feet. They do not really understand what they are treading on at all. If you are evangelizing an unbeliever, they will not know what blasphemy they are uttering. According to Ephesians 2:1-3, their entire conduct is offensive to God.

Paul even regretted some of the words he himself uttered about Jesus Christ. In 1 Timothy 1:12-16 he says, "I thank Christ Jesus our Lord, who has given me strength, that he considered me faithful, appointing me to his service. Even though I was once a blasphemer and a persecutor and a violent man, I was shown mercy because I acted in ignorance and unbelief. The grace of our Lord was poured out on me abundantly, along with the faith and love that are in Christ Jesus. Here is a trustworthy saying that deserves full acceptance: Christ Jesus came into the world to save sinners - of whom I am the worst. But for that very reason I was shown mercy so that in me, the worst of sinners, Christ Jesus might display his unlimited patience as an example for those who would believe on him and receive eternal life."

You try to caution this individual, but if you're witnessing don't be surprised if they tread on something blasphemous if they are not a believer. You must have straint. Unfortunately, they don't know the precious truth upon which they are treading.

BEFRIEND THEM

In 2 John 9-10, we read about how to maintain a standard of limited courtesies toward those who refuse the gospel. These verses speak about sharing the gospel with someone who is hostile to the teachings of the gospel. How do you know when it is time to stop talking to those who have rejected the gospel time and time again? Our advice is this: When you have said all that you can say, they know the script, they know everything you are going say, and they still remain hostile – then, you have done your part. Continue to pray for them, and begin sharing with others whose hearts are ready to receive the truth. Of course, if they still have honest questions, then continue the discussion and ask the Lord to direct your conversations.

Matthew 10:14 speaks to those who are hostile to the truth; not to those sincerely seeking, "If anyone will not welcome you or listen to your words, shake the dust off your feet when you leave that home or town." Likewise,

Luke gives the following account in Acts 13:50-51, "But the Jews incited the God-fearing women of high standing and the leading men of the city. They stirred up persecution against Paul and Barnabas, and expelled them from their region. So they shook the dust from their feet in protest against them and went to Iconium."

Also notice another verse that addresses the same concept. It says not to bid them "godspeed" (2 John verse11, KJV). This term means that you should not extend to hostile unbelievers the small and seemingly insignificant accolades that we often extend to other believers. For example, I (Ben) will personally send an email to a believer with a phrase like "God Bless," then type my name. But when I know that I am emailing an unbeliever, I will politely conclude the email with "Sincerely" or "Hope you have a great day." To share meaningful spiritual encouragements with unbelievers may very well make them content with how they are spiritually – all the while they remain lost and in their sinful state. Until they accept what you share, there is still a distinction between all who are saved and those who are lost (2 John 9-10).

TAKE TIME TO LISTEN

It is so important that we take time to rehearse what the specific and necessary biblical truths are so that we are biblically accurate. But we must also take time with the same level of scrutiny to assess and listen to the life situation of the person with whom we are sharing the gospel. Then we can better measure what words will minister most effectively to the heart of the one receiving the message. After rehearsing all of these biblical principles related to tact, people skills and the means by which to share these principles, remember the time tested, universal teachings that the Bible provides for us that encourage us to be mindful of the life story of those we meet. For example, Colossians 4:5 comes to mind where it encourages us to "Be wise in the way you act toward outsiders; make the most of every opportunity."

Another verse that encourages us to use various approaches for different personalities is 1 Thessalonians 5:14, "And we urge you, brothers, warn those who are idle, encourage the timid, help the weak, be patient with everyone."

Think about all the people in your life who have carefully framed their words to help you understand a concept, the error of your ways, or have given a soft correction or tender rebuke. And they have done it in such a way that their thoughtfulness and consideration left your heart encouraged instead of crushed! They helped turn what could have been a horrible, painful memory into a time of learning, growing, and thankfulness. We are blessed to have these people in our lives, and we can be a blessing in return as we remember to present the biggest love story to the world in the same spirit.

WALK IN GRACE

My (Ben's) father was a self-trained pastor. He was so passionate about ministry. I remember watching him give counsel every Sunday – after his Sunday School class and after the church service when people came down to the altar. I was so impressed with his genuine concern for people. I wanted to be that type of person that was able to give godly advice. He listened so patiently, he comforted with such tenderness, and his transparency endeared him to his congregation. When I observed his ministry, I knew it would take me years to develop his gift. I wanted to be like my father.

A few years down the road, I was contemplating Bible schools for college, and I was invited to a meet and greet for potential freshmen at a school close to where I lived in Michigan. The president of the college stood up and shared a verse that will forever stick with me. "But sanctify the Lord God in your hearts, and always be ready to give a defense to everyone who asks you a reason for the hope that is in you, with meekness and fear" (1 Peter 3:15). I thought to myself, that's what I want! That is the biblical sentence that articulates exactly what my heart has always desired. I've always wanted to give guidance to people so that they would know how to live. Based on biblical truth, I wanted to help people experience comfort in times of need. I wanted them to know that I genuinely cared for them. And I also wanted them to feel equipped and empowered to do the work of the ministry.

That was my heart's desire, but I thought there was no way I could achieve this level of ministry. I assumed you had to be smart, you had to have degrees, and you had to know the languages of the Bible to counsel people in the right direction. Not so, according to this verse. And not so according to the passage I will refer to in this chapter. You will see that any man or any woman who follows the prescriptions given from this passage can give spiritual counsel to anyone.

SERVE OTHERS

Before we can talk about evangelistic efforts and how to articulate our faith to others, we must first focus on the condition of our own hearts. You see, if we are not in line with the Holy Spirit, our efforts will be empty and ultimately fruitless.

I (Ben) recently had an individual approach me, and I remember vividly what he said, "If someone needs to get on fire for God, wouldn't it be beneficial to get him involved in ministry or in a leadership role? Then he could taste and see that the Lord is good!" The first thing that came to my mind was, "No – not a good idea!" But I restrained myself. When this question was raised, the person was essentially saying that it might be profitable to put someone in a church "doing" position in order to get his or her heart fired up for God. I believe that's a prescription for failure because it's in reverse order. Scripture makes it very clear that prior to doing the work of ministry, first our hearts must be spiritually prepared.

In Acts 6:3 we see where the disciples were instructed by the twelve disciples to meet the needs of widows. They stated, "Brothers, choose seven men from among you who are known to be full of the Spirit and wisdom. We will turn this responsibility over to them." Prior to dealing with the business at hand, the men needed to be spiritual, controlled, and in line with God. Before they could "do," their hearts needed to "be" ready.

I also think of 2 Timothy 2:2 where Paul says to Timothy, "And the things you have heard me say in the presence of many witnesses entrust to reliable men who will also be qualified to teach others." In other words, "Don't commit these things in order to make them faithful, but find men who are committed, who are spiritually mature and then commit these things to them." Paul wanted the mentors to find mentees who were already somewhat mature – men who saw their need for spiritual growth.

By examining these passages we see that today's Christians need to be similarly prepared to do ministry. Therefore, we don't want to jump right into evangelism without first addressing who we should be. This is a very important element of Christian service.

I (Ben) was told at the first Bible college I attended that our personal devotion time should be comprised of material outside of our class studies, and we were encouraged to take time to talk to godly men who could influence our walk with Christ. One author of more than forty books who came to our school (the late John Wolford) made this statement, "I do not find myself getting the most out of God's Word unless I'm preparing to write a book, or preparing to preach a sermon or a lesson." He was saying, "If I'm not studying for a purpose, it's hard to get something out of it." I agreed with him that I should make my studies my devotion, studying for knowledge, application and life-change.

For you, I think the Lord has seen fit to expose you to the subjects of personal spiritual growth and evangelism at this particular time in your life. I pray that you will be able to use your times in God's Word as a tool to develop personal devotion and to examine your heart. In fact, if your mind is truly meditating on these spiritual truths, I believe you will learn great ways to apply these principles to your life as your heart is infused with His precious Word. But the absolute best way to earn a hearing with anyone is to practice what you preach!

BEFORE I DO, I MUST BE

There are many misconceptions about what a godly person is. Many people refer to others as being "spiritual." For example, sometimes students recommend a girl to a friend as a potential date because "she's really a godly person." Or you may hear someone say, "You ought to consider dating him because he really loves the Lord." However, it is a likely possibility that the person being recommended is not a godly person in the true sense.

We are going to search God's Word to find a clear description of a godly person. As believers who desire to be holy before God, we need to make sure we understand how God defines a "godly person."

MISCONCEPTIONS ABOUT BEING A GODLY PERSON

They Have Biblical Training (Isaiah 29:13)

Some people describe a godly person as one who has received formal Bible training. Let's look at Isaiah 29:13, "The Lord says: "These people come near to me with their mouth and honor me with their lips, but their hearts are far from me. Their worship of me is made up only of rules taught by men." Let me paraphrase: "They know a lot about Me and do lip service to Me, but their hearts are moved away from Me because their worship of Me is made up only of rules taught by men." Literally, they have learned God's precepts by empty rote memorization and have essentially flash-carded God's attributes to death without their heart being linked in devotion to Him.

Many people sit through years of Sunday school classes; they know the stories in their heads, but they do not apply them to their hearts. They may have perfect church attendance, they may have earned badges and memorized verses, but these disciplines usually will not produce a godly person in and of themselves. It's all for show. According to Isaiah, the truths of God must be received into the heart and then lived out, regardless of any formal biblical training.

I (Ben) was at a men's retreat in Jonesboro, Georgia with a fellow pastor, talking about integrity and purity among the men there. In a Q&A session, one of the men asked, "How is it that some pastors who preach the Word week in and week out can fall into adultery?" I responded, "I believe it's often because those pastors prepare sermons in second and third person. They say 'he' must do this, 'the church' must do that, and 'you' must do this. But prior to preaching, he needs to speak it in first person. He must say, 'I' must do this, or how can 'I' conform my life to this portion of God's Word?" Pastors and trained Bible students will fail when their training and preparation is not internalized. When they just go through the motions to prepare a sermon, it ends up being all for show. You see, if you tout how many books and volumes you have on your shelf but your heart is not holy, then the books are mere showpieces. So we see that it is not biblical training that necessarily prepares a person to be "godly." So it must be something else.

They Attend Church (Matthew 7)

In Matthew chapter 7:22-23 we read that on Judgment Day, "Many will say to me on that day, 'Lord, Lord, did we not prophesy in your name, and in your name drive out demons and perform many miracles?'" Notice that many of the things they named off were good things that they did for God. I know this passage is somewhat debatable because some say these people are believers, while some say they are not. If they are believers, they've done incredibly spiritual things: performing miracles, casting out demons, etc. Yet, the Bible says, "Then I will tell them plainly, 'I never knew you. Away from me, you evildoers!'"

Some suggest these people are unbelievers who hung around in church and knew how to use the Christian vernacular in an attempt to persuade God to let them into heaven. They "talk the talk" but it's all empty. Regardless of who these individuals are, we see through their example that we must achieve more than a mere intellectual understanding of God; we must have more than just a cognitive knowledge of Him. There is a saying that twenty percent of the church does eighty percent of the work. We typically view the twenty percent as godly people, but a godly person must be about more than just work.

In the Third Epistle of John, we see the story of a guy named Diotrephes. John says in 3 John verse 9, "I wrote to the church, but Diotrephes, who loves to be first, will have nothing to do with us." We don't know if this man was a pastor or not, but we know he wanted to be; he wanted to be the leader.

In Colossians 1:18, we are told that Jesus Christ "is the head of the body, the church; he is the beginning and the firstborn from among the dead, so that in everything he might have the supremacy." If you want first place in your church solely for your own glory, you're going toe-to-toe with Jesus Christ. And so we see that Diotrephes was off track. Deeds performed in church or profound actions do not gain prominence with God.

In Matthew 13 we read the parable of the four soils. Seed is thrown on soil and some of it takes root and is then snatched away. Some hits bedrock and dies. Some is trampled on and there is no growth. And some hits the fine soil. The first three examples of soil represent non-believers. In like manner, some people show the likeness of a true believer, but they have no true grounding so that when things get tough, they wither away.

They Have Spiritual Parents

Another misconception is that if we have spiritual parents we too will be automatically spiritual. I (Ben) recall after my wife and I got married, she was sharing the gospel with a woman who was not a believer yet. She said, "Oh, I'm going to heaven." My wife replied, "Really? How do you know you're on your way to heaven?" The woman said, "Because my mother washes the parish priest's robes every week, and it takes a very special person to do this." My wife found her response sad as she was relying on her mother to gain spirituality.

In Philippians 3:4-5, Paul addressed this type of belief when he said, "If anyone else thinks he has reasons to put confidence in the flesh, I have more: circumcised on the eighth day, of the people of Israel, of the tribe of Benjamin, a Hebrew of Hebrews; in regard to the law, a Pharisee. " This is a comment about his family and their wealth and standing in the Jewish community. The best teacher in Tarsus, Gamaliel, educated him. But then Paul goes on to say, "But whatever was to my profit I now consider loss for the sake of Christ" (Philippians 3:7).

Paul considered and weighed the worth of all that he had and all that he was and, like an accountant weighing assets and liabilities, he no longer considered them an asset. To Paul, they were of no worth in comparison to knowing Christ. So as we are weighing these different things – biblical training, church attendance, and spiritual parents – we need to continue our biblical search for the description of a godly person because these things do not make a person godly in and of themselves.

In Ephesians 4:1-3 we find some insights into what makes a godly person. "I ... urge you to live a life worthy of the calling you have received. Be completely humble and gentle; be patient, bearing with one another in love. Make every effort to keep the unity of the Spirit through the bond of peace."

And later in the same chapter we read, "Get rid of all bitterness, rage and anger, brawling and slander, along with every form of malice. Be kind and compassionate to one another, forgiving each other, just as in Christ God forgave you" (Ephesians 4:31-32). "

Set your minds on things above, not on earthly things . . . Do not lie to each other . . . clothe yourselves with compassion, kindness, humility, gentleness and patience. Bear with each other and forgive whatever grievances you may have against one another. Forgive as the Lord forgave you. And over all these virtues put on love . . . Let the peace of Christ rule in your hearts . . . And be thankful. Let the word of Christ dwell in you richly" (Colossians 3:2, 9, 12-16).

If these were the only guidelines we found in God's Word about being a "godly person," we wouldn't lack for information! But there is much more within the pages of Scripture on this topic. It would be a helpful exercise to look for additional verses that bring clarity to the definition of a godly person – according to God's Word. Looking at another source, The International Standard Bible Encyclopedia defines a godly person as "a person who is self-disciplined in godly attitudes and habits!"

The only way we can be self-disciplined in godly attitudes and habits is to learn about God, His Word, and His Church through biblical education and training. A godly person is one who takes the truth of God's Word and consistently lives it out day-by-day, from the heart, being careful to obey it.

AN ANALOGY

You're sitting in church, listening to a sermon on Luke 7. In the middle of this chapter, you hear a story about a funeral procession wherein a widow is burying her only son. The preacher reminds you that in Jewish culture this woman is in the most despairing situation because if you are a widow and you have lost your only son, this means you have no males to protect or support you. You further learn that this is why a great company from the town is with her. You hear that Jesus walks up to this woman and says, "Don't cry." Your intellect is spurred a little bit; you're stimulated intellectually by all of these little facts. You conclude: "I've learned something new. I've been fed. Therefore, I'm spiritual!" No way. You've just learned some biblical facts that have stimulated you intellectually.

And then consider Jesus' words to the widow, "Don't cry." And you think, in tough times I don't have to cry because Christ is with me and will take care of things. You say, "I've made an application and drafted the application.

Therefore, I'm spiritual!" Nope. You've simply made a logical deduction. So you continue to forge an opinion, "When times get tough I will trust Christ. Great—I've more than applied this truth. I have prepared myself for the reaction I should have. Therefore, I'm spiritual!" No, again. You have simply added another "go to" reaction on the flow chart of your mind.

Here is the proper application. When times are tough, you trust Him. You run into another tough time, and you trust Him. Yet another tough time comes, and you still proclaim, "I have seen the goodness of God, and I will continue to trust Him. I know He is always with me. He is good and kind and loving and merciful and compassionate and has never winked at my plight; He has never slumbered at my request. I will and I must trust Him again and again – no matter how difficult life becomes." That is the committed faith of a person who is selfdisciplined in godly attitudes and habits. Job said, "Though He slay me, yet will I trust Him" (Job 13:15, NKJV).

You may be like many Christians. When tough times come, there's an inner battle. Tough times come and you struggle within yourself and think, "Why am I struggling like this?" A truly godly person is someone who is self-disciplined, whose default reaction says, "I will follow God's way, no matter what."

Allow me (Ben) to share a personal note. Let me tell you what I do when the Evil One comes with his temptations. I know my flesh well enough to know that I cannot battle against these temptations by myself. My flesh needs an insertion of truth that cuts through my own faulty logic and limitations. So when I face temptation or I struggle spiritually, I often say aloud, "God's way – God's way – God's way!"

And as I'm saying this, I slowly begin to see through new eyes. I have learned that our flesh will not want to pursue righteousness. Therefore, we must defeat the cravings of sin before they take root within us. And so in my own weakness, I call out to my Lord by claiming "God's way" over and over. In so doing, I disrupt the flow of the flesh. This is my personal act of self-discipline, as I call on God to help me avoid temptation. A two-fold way to becoming a godly person is: (1) recognize your weakness amid temptation (2) call on God, maybe even verbally, when you are struggling with temptation, or discouragement, or disbelief. I pray you always live life God's way – God's way – God's way!

A LOOK AT YOUR OWN HEART – PSALM 139 (NKJV)

It is vitally important that we take critical looks at our own hearts from time to time. In the eyes of many, one of the most beautiful Psalms is Psalm 139. It provides guidance in the examination of our hearts. Verses 1-6 read: "O Lord, You have searched me and known me. You know my sitting down and my rising up; You understand my thought afar off. You comprehend my path and my lying down, and are acquainted with all my ways. For there is not a word on my tongue, but behold, O Lord, You know it altogether. You have hedged me behind and before, and laid Your hand upon me. Such knowledge is too wonderful for me; it is high, I cannot attain it."

Verse 1—You've searched me and known me

Verse 2—You know my sitting down and my rising up;

You understand my thoughts

Verse 3—You comprehend my path,

You are acquainted with all my ways

Verse 4—There is not a word on my tongue, but Lord,

You know it altogether.

Verse 6—Such knowledge is too wonderful for me.

Then in verses 7-12, David speaks of God's omnipresence. He says, "Where can I go from Your spirit? Or where can I flee from Your presence?"

Verse 8—If I make my bed in hell, behold, You are there.

Verse 9—If I take (and listen to the Jewish mindset here, the figurative language) the wings of the morning (as quick as the morning creeps up on us), and dwell (or I shoot) in the uttermost parts of the sea, even there Your hand shall lead me, and Your right hand shall hold me.

In the geography of the Jewish nation of Jerusalem, the sun rises in the east and to their west is the Mediterranean Sea. So to say as quick as the wings of the morning comes (east), and I shoot in the farthest corner of the sea (west), even there Your hand leads me and Your right hand will hold me.

Verse 11—If I say, 'Surely the darkness shall fall on me,
even the night shall be light about me;

Verse 12—Indeed, the darkness shall not hide from You, but the night shines as the day; The darkness and the light are both alike to You.

Not being able to hide from God shouldn't be a scary thing. The fact that God knows you through and through should be reassuring to you. I remember in elementary school, if I had a bad report card I was fearful. But bringing home a positive report card for my parents was exciting. Likewise, if our lives are holy, we welcome God fully knowing us. Conversely, if our life has sin in it, then, it's a scary thing. Like John says, "God is light and in him there is no darkness at all" (1 John 1:5). A godly person begs to be transparent and loves God's scrutiny. Your spiritual stability is in direct proportion to how you view God. Verses 13-16 talk about God's omnipotence; the fact that God is all powerful.

Verse 13—For You have formed my inward parts; You have covered me (or knitted me together) in my mother's womb.

Verse 14—I will praise You, for I am fearfully and wonderfully made;

Marvelous are Your works, and that my soul knows very well.

Verse 15—My frame was not hidden from You, when I was made in secret, and skillfully wrought in the lowest parts of the earth.

Verse 16—Your eyes saw my substance, being yet unformed.

And in Your book they all were written, the days fashioned for me, when as yet there were none of them.

Verse 17—How precious also are Your thoughts to me, O God!

How great is the sum of them!

Verse 18—If I should count them, they would be more in number than the sand. When I awake, I am still with You

Verse 19—Oh, that You would slay the wicked, O God!

Depart from Me, therefore, you bloodthirsty men.

Verse 20—For they speak against You wickedly;

Your enemies take Your name in vain.

Verse 21—Do I not hate them, O Lord, who hate You?

And do I not loathe those who rise up against You?

Verse 22—I hate them with perfect hatred; I count them my enemies."

You think, "Whoa, that's not a psalm of love!" It is important to see that David is saying (paraphrased), "You are a great God that knows all and is everywhere and is so powerful. Your thoughts of us are numerous, even more than the granules of sand on the beach." And David continues, "I love You, and it grieves me when people don't love You like I do." He's literally saying, "Please, as You look upon me, see me differently than You do those who blaspheme You. I don't want anything to do with those who blaspheme You. I don't want to be in their company."

Psalm 1:1-2 says, "Blessed is the man who does not walk in the counsel of the wicked or stand in the way of sinners or sit in the seat of mockers. But his delight is in the law of the LORD, and on his law he meditates day and night." I don't want anything in my life that will align me with such people, and I want to separate everything I do from those that blaspheme God. I want to protect my Christian reputation.

Then Psalm 139 ends with, "Search me, O God, and know my heart; try me, and know my anxieties; And see if there is any wicked way in me, and lead me in the way everlasting" (Psalm 139:23-24, NKJV).

A WILLING SUBMISSION TO HIS WAYS

In Psalm 139:1, David makes the statement, "Lord, You have searched me and known me." Why in the world, if God has searched him and has known him in verse 1, does David then ask God to please search him and know his heart in verse 23? Hasn't God already done this? Doesn't that seem somewhat odd? This is the sign of a strong spiritual man because David is expressing a willing submission to God's ways – all the time. He is saying, "God, I know You already do this, but I want to show You that I'm going to go with You willingly, and I welcome You to search my heart."

When police officers come to the point where they have to take an individual into custody, they ask, "Are you going to cooperate with us or do we have to take you by force?" This is the same concept. God searches us. He knows us, but He wants us to cooperate with Him with a heart that says, "You are a good God; You know me, and I want to know You" (Philippians 3:10, paraphrased). We must welcome His presence and His searching of our hearts. I want to know God and I want to say to Him, "I'm going to go with You everywhere." That is the heart that is willing and open to Christ.

Ask yourself, "Am I a godly person?" The answer lies in how you answer these two questions: Am I willing to go God's way? Am I willing to open my heart to Him at all times? In light of these same questions, are you a godly person? How valuable is your relationship with Him? Is it precious enough that you are a selfdisciplined person with godly attitudes and habits?

CHAPTER **ELEVEN**

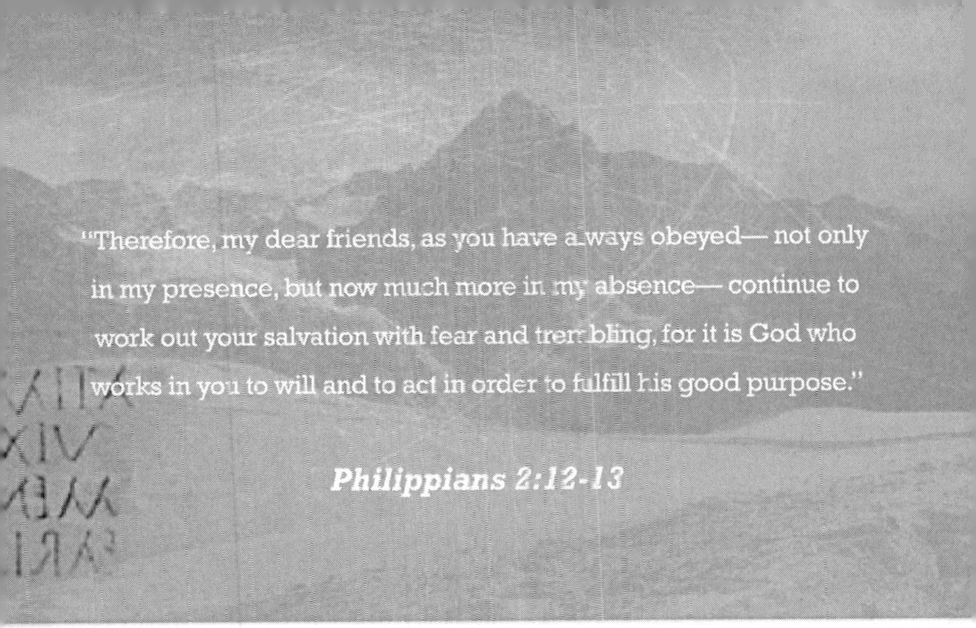

"Therefore, my dear friends, as you have always obeyed— not only in my presence, but now much more in my absence— continue to work out your salvation with fear and trembling, for it is God who works in you to will and to act in order to fulfill his good purpose."

Philippians 2:12-13

WALK YOUR TALK

We have spent some time in the previous chapters discussing how to enter into a relationship with Jesus Christ, how to cultivate that relationship, and how to share the wonderful story of His grace and love with others. But we would be remiss if we didn't share how to practically live out these principles in your day-to-day life.

Without the addition of these practical recommendations, it would be like a lecture that fails to explain how the teachings of the discipline can be integrated into the real world. Or like a pastor, who after he elucidates the most acute, profound points of a theological doctrine, fails to show how that very truth is able to affect the daily lives of those in his congregation.

What follows are some practical suggestions on how you can live out the spiritual teachings found in this book. Practice them regularly. Remain sensitive to the Holy Spirit's guidance on how to pray during your practice of these spiritual activities. And be careful never to forget that you need to apply these activities with your whole heart, not simply mechanically check them off your "to do" list.

Please note that the following recommendations make the assumption that you have, indeed, committed your life to Jesus Christ as your Lord and Savior, and that you adhere to a Biblical/Christian Worldview in the daily decisions of your life.

KNOW WHAT YOU BELIEVE

Begin by asking a believing friend to pose some questions – as if he or she is an unbeliever who is sincerely seeking to know what the Bible says about the truth of salvation in Jesus Christ.

Here are some questions you should be prepared to answer:

1. Why do I need to be saved?
2. Is everyone in need of salvation?
3. Can I save myself?
4. Can I approach God assuming that He will give me – a nice, respectful person – a "pass" and not hold me to the same level of spiritual scrutiny that He holds other people to?
5. What is God's role in saving my soul?
6. Is everyone automatically saved since Jesus died and rose again?
7. Is having a cognitive knowledge of biblical truths enough to be saved?
8. What is the difference between "cognitive" knowledge and "volitional" knowledge of these saving truths?
9. Create your own additional questions that you believe would help you retain and comprehend what you have learned in these chapters.

And be prepared for one more thing. After one of these initial questions, assume that your friend will follow up with this question, "How do you know that?" This will require that you thoroughly understand the Bible references that you quote to your friend when responding to the initial questions.

Now, turn the tables and you play the role of the inquiring unbeliever and have your friend respond to these questions. You may think that your friend has it easier because he/she just heard your response, but this is not always the case. Knowing the concept and hearing the concept audibly is one thing, but clearly verbalizing the concept to a friend in a concise fashion is very challenging.

When you understand the basic tenets of the gospel message, you ought to prepare a mini salvation presentation. For example, pretend that you are walking in a parking lot and meet an acquaintance or friend. You find yourself walking together into the building. You both walk through the lobby and approach the elevator. Right as you enter the elevator, your friend, knowing you are a Christian, asks you, "Hey, could you tell me what it means to be saved?" In this scenario, you have twelve floors and approximately 45-60 seconds to share the gospel – as long as no one else gets on the elevator for those twelve floors. This is indeed the ideal time to share your previously prepared, mini salvation presentation.

Here are some suggestions:

1. Write out the essential elements that absolutely must be communicated concerning salvation.

2. Decide what can be discussed in a follow-up conversation. That is, determine what details are not essential to the initial salvation presentation. You don't want to get too far ahead of yourself and confuse the issue.

3. Rehearse this presentation with a friend. The goal is to have a well-prepared, well-thought-out, sincere presentation.

4. Go out with a friend and look for 45-60 second opportunities. I know that may sound strange but remember, in today's society, time is precious, and people are not normally going to make a major decision in 45- 60 seconds. Look at this as a first step in the witnessing process. Others will water the seed you have planted, and God will bring the increase. Who knows, 45 seconds may turn into 45 minutes, and God may provide you with the incredible blessing of seeing a spiritual miracle occur right in front of your eyes!

5. Now, for the biggest challenge. Convert this 45-60 second presentation into the language of a four-year-old without skewing or omitting any truth. Be vivid, imaginative, patient, and very prepared. Consider it a victory if they are able to grasp only one piece of the salvation puzzle during your conversation. Rehearse this a few times introducing new information each time until it becomes natural, and you are at ease with it. God will use it to illuminate the mind by the work of the Spirit in another person's soul. As lecturers,we have never understood why, traditionally, we adults have made instructional times so boring. You will find that a childlike presentation works well for adults when it comes to the salvation message.

In addition to these activities, rehearse your own thoughts and reflections about your personal salvation story that you could include in your presentation. As the Apostle John encourages us in Revelation 2:5, "Remember the height from which you have fallen!" It is good to dwell, not on the sin and damage done, but on the miraculous delivery God has provided in our lives. And there is no greater deliverance than that of God's salvation of our souls.

WALK CLOSE

We would encourage you to read the parable in Luke 15:4-7 regarding the shepherd who was missing one of his sheep. Notice that the shepherd leaves the 99 sheep to go look for the one sheep. That's a picture of how important each individual person is to Jesus, our Good Shepherd. When just one of us wanders off to do our own thing, He's aware. His desire is for that one to come back into the sheepfold.

And look at verses 5 and 6, "And when he finds it, he joyfully puts it on his shoulders and goes home." There doesn't seem to be a big "aha" in that statement, but there's more than meets the eye in those two verses. In studying the culture of shepherds and sheep, we find the reason for why the shepherd put the lost sheep on his shoulders. It was the practice of shepherds to break the wayward sheep's leg and carry the sheep close to him until the leg healed. After the leg had healed, the sheep was less likely to wander off again because during that time of healing, the sheep had been close enough to hear the shepherd's heartbeat. The lost sheep now trusted his shepherd.

In your own heart, recall the moments that you have no doubt in your mind that God used in your life "to break your leg" – to turn you off a path of sin and protect you from a life of deep regret. Take a moment to thank the Lord for taking you off that wayward path. Talk to the Lord and tell Him how things are going now in your life. Have you gotten back on the same path of sin, or are you now living a life that is honoring to God? If you are on the same path of sin, confess it immediately and passionately to God, and commit to pursue a life based on biblical truth.

In addition, find a friend or two who are committed to pursue a Biblical/Christian worldview in the details of life. Surround yourself with those who will encourage you to honor the Lord in every area of your life. Engage in spiritual discussions with them. Talk about the Scriptures with them. Pray with them. Worship with them. Socialize with them. And, remember, even strong Christians are still human, and they will make mistakes and poor choices. So, if someone lets you down spiritually, remember that your hope is not in a person, but your hope and encouragement is found in the Lord. Remember, it comes down to your own commitment, passion and love for the Lord Jesus Christ. You must be willing to allow the Holy Spirit to guide your life.

We cannot grow in our faith or effectively share our faith without regularly reading and studying the Bible. So we'd like to suggest another passage of Scripture for you to investigate on your own, Luke 15:8-10. This parable (story) follows the one about the lost sheep. A parable takes a commonplace incident, a natural occurrence, and uses it to illustrate a spiritual point, a universal truth. This story is about a woman who had ten silver coins and lost one of them. At that time in history, each of those silver coins was the equivalent to a day's wage. The longer her coin was lost, the less probable it was that it would be found because it could easily be covered with dust and swept out the door the next day.

After reading this second parable, what do you think Jesus is trying to get across to His listeners—and to us—in these two parables? When you read verses in the Bible, remember to use the critical thinking skills we've talked about. Ask yourself questions regarding the passage. To get you started, let's think through what you know so far. The first question is easy. Did you see any relationship between these two parables? Both the shepherd and the woman lost something. Any other similarities? They both went the extra mile to look for the lost items; there was an urgency to find them. Anything else? There was much rejoicing when they were found.

Now that you've gained a bit of knowledge about these texts, the next question to ask is, "So what?" "What do these verses have to do with me? I'm not a shepherd, and I haven't lost any money recently." If you put down your Bible before you ask and answer the "So What?" question, you've just added cognitive knowledge to your brain. And remember, we've already stated in multiple ways that cognitive knowledge is not enough. It's the application of truth, the volitional will, that transforms us to be more like Christ as we interact with people on a daily basis. It's been said that "Knowledge puffs up, but application bursts the bubble!" When you study the Bible, that's a great quote to remember.

Let's get back to the

that both of these parables

one of us. Take that truth and

(those who have yet to trust Ch

about sharing the truth of God's

mile to contact them? Am I willing

in a spiritual conversation? Have I

give me the opportunity to present th

honestly before you read on.

What's another answer to the "

much rejoicing when the lost sheep and ...ound. That is a picture of how God rejoices each and ev... time someone embraces His truth and joins the family of God. Take a few moments and try to imagine how you would feel if you had the opportunity to share your faith and lead someone to believe and trust in Christ. What a privilege and what joy would be yours—to know that particular person will be in eternity with you, forever.

So how are you doing in your day-in and day-out interactions with your friends and families? Does your walk match your talk? How do your actions communicate who you profess to be? Go through your past week (at work, school, the gym, after hours, in the mornings, on the athletic field, etc.), and ask yourself if your decisions, attitudes, words, body language, emails, responses or your failure to respond, etc. caused others around you to think positively of you. More so, did your actions point others to the fact that you are a Christian, and did your responses foster positive comments from them? Did you hear anything like the following remarks? "You did not react like other people typically do." "Thank you for being so kind." "Wow, the others took the news in a totally different way than you. I really appreciate your positive attitude."

If you were able to point to positive experiences, then take a moment to thank God for the opportunity to spread the goodness of God through your actions. Then ask God to give you more opportunities to testify of His goodness [illegible] you had not demonstrated a Christ- [illegible] a moment to apologize to Jesus for not [illegible] of His goodness. Identify the sin(s) that you [illegible] you feeling that you have every right to act or feel in [illegible] way you did. Then ask the Lord for an opportunity to testify [illegible] odness this coming week – as a way to show Him that you are [illegible] about your commitment to look like a true believer in your daily walk.

There is a third parable that follows the first two we've already discussed. Set aside some time to read and reflect on Luke 15:11-32. Ask some of your friends to join you in looking at this parable, and then get together to share your ideas and talk about any questions that might have come up in your study. Don't forget to ask the "So what?" question. It will be interesting to see how many "So what's?" the group comes up with!

One "So what?" we don't want you to miss in this parable is to consider when the Lord gave you a second chance. Consider the people in your life who showed you the mercy of the Lord and made it possible for you to get back up again spiritually. Think about the words they used and the amount of time they took to talk to you about getting on the right path. Consider the time commitment and emotional battle that took place in their hearts to confront you regarding your sin. As you do, thank God for their courage, love, and commitment to your wellbeing. Ask yourself how their actions and their commitment to you reflected the last two verses of the Book of James, "My brothers, if one of you should wander from the truth and someone should bring him back, remember this: Whoever turns a sinner from the error of his way will save him from death and cover over a multitude of sins" (James 5:19-20) In addition, consider how their actions kept a multitude of sins from occurring in your life. Take a moment to thank God for that encounter, and if possible, thank them again.

Try taking some time to analyze and discuss a recent sermon from your pastor and/or a teaching lesson that you and your friends have recently heard. Discuss if the topic was directed to unbelievers, believers or both. What was said or not said that made you come to this conclusion? If it's both, how do you think the unbelieving attendees received the material presented? Would they have understood the teaching of the gospel clearly or was it too veiled? What could have been included to give more clarity for the unbelievers to understand the gospel presentation?

Remember, when you analyze and critique a sermon or a teaching lesson, you should always be positive and supportive of the one who proclaimed the truth, and realize that not every sermon has to speak to both believers and unbelievers. Never forget that the Lord leads presenters of the gospel to direct their comments in one way or another, so do not be quick to conclude that a particular sermon was imbalanced if it did not speak to both believers and unbelievers. Simply do this exercise as an observation exercise.

Search the Scriptures to see if there is another teaching lesson by Jesus and/or the apostles that was directed both to believers and unbelievers. The Gospels (Matthew, Mark, Luke, John) and the Book of Acts may be a good place to look for these teaching lessons. Discuss the components that you believe were directed to believers as well as the teachings that were directed to unbelievers. After you discuss some of these passages with a friend or two, possibly think about how you would share one of these passages with a mixed audience of believers and unbelievers. What would the title of your talk be? What points would you emphasize? How would you wrap up your teaching lesson? Note: a good source to guide you may be your pastor or someone who has had experience juggling the dynamics of a multi-interest audience.

WALK GUARDED

Living out your faith on a daily basis is not a life for wimps! The Bible describes Christians as soldiers, and we are called to put on our spiritual armor to withstand the assaults from Satan. "Put on the full armor of God so that you can take your stand against the devil's schemes" (Ephesians 6:11).

We are assured of ultimate victory at the end of the story. But for now, the enemy's goal is to trip up believers so they will succumb to temptation and the name of Jesus will be tarnished. The Ephesians passage continues, "And pray in the Spirit on all occasions with all kinds of prayers and requests. With this in mind, be alert and always keep on praying for all the saints" (Ephesians 6:18). In order to "walk guarded," begin praying every single morning – without fail – the words that I (Ben) pray myself,

> Lord, as I start my day with You, please keep me sensitive to the very baby steps of sin. Make me be able to sense when I am beginning down this digression of sin. And if so, give me the wisdom to turn and run toward You in honesty, confession, and with a love for You and Your righteousness. I want righteousness to dictate the terms in my life today!

Now, when I find myself having to confess to God that I had been insensitive to the baby steps of sin on that particular day, I make sure I pray this prayer to Him once again. The point being, make sure you are in constant communion with the Lord regarding your spiritual challenges, so that you catch your sin early before it permeates your entire heart and mind.

Begin a brief search of the Scriptures that speak to God providing victory over sin. After you find these Scriptures, call a friend and share the verse(s) with him/her. Ask them to share their thoughts, then pray together and ask the Lord to give you the wisdom to obey Him, so that you will always experience victory in your own life.

After you do this, commit to memorize one verse at a time. Then, ask God to provide the opportunity for you to share the truth of these verses with another person who may be in need of hearing about how he/she can experience God's victory. Repeat this process throughout the coming days, weeks, and months. This type of spiritual activity is the purest form of providing spiritual edification to our fellow brothers and sisters in Christ.

Building on the previous recommended spiritual activity, I want to encourage you to embark on what may initially sound like a scary endeavor. That is, I want you to take one of the verses that you find in your research and begin to prepare to teach both the meaning and application of it to someone else. Let me pause here and explain what I mean by teach. Don't always default to thinking of a pastor or professor when you think about being taught. When you teach someone something, it often is done outside of a classroom or pulpit – it is done as you are living life together. Teaching occurs when you give advice while sipping coffee on a park bench, while you walk down a sidewalk with a friend, or while you sit in a softball team's dugout waiting to take the field, etc. Teaching happens whenever a person elaborates on the meaning of a particular verse and how it applies in their life. In fact, having these discussions as you are living life with a friend is the essence of teaching.

So, I want you to focus on a verse. Study what it says, do a little more digging and read the surrounding context of the verse (possibly read the whole chapter), and then search out an occasion to teach it to someone else. I would recommend that you ask a friend if you can try your thoughts out on them to see if they are clear and understandable. I think you will find their questions will help you know what aspects of the verse need to be presented more clearly. Receiving his/her feedback will also tip you off to what is important to the listener and most likely future audiences. After you share it with your friend, consider their feedback, and find another person to share your thoughts with regarding the passage.

WALK IN GRACE

If you search deep down in your heart and find yourself in an unhealthy spiritual state, consider following some of the advice from James, Chapter 5. Read this chapter and find all of the ways you can apply to your life what you read. What does it mean to you personally when James says, "You too, be patient and stand firm, because the Lord's coming is near."? Think about the last time you grumbled and complained about something or someone. What would have been different in your attitude or actions if you had followed James' warning, "Don't grumble against each other."? Or what about the reference to Elijah and his prayer life? What do you know about Elijah? And what does his prayer have to do with your life today? Choose someone to dive into a spiritual discussion with about what James teaches in just this one chapter.

Next, begin to list very practical things that can be done every day of your week to strengthen you spiritually. Then ask a very close, trustworthy, honest friend who demonstrates personal holiness for their opinion on what you wrote down. Possibly they can suggest other spiritual activities to add to your list.

Also choose a few friends with whom you can have varying levels of spiritual conversations. You could start your day on Monday morning with an encouraging spiritual discussion over coffee and breakfast with a friend. The conversation may simply be about what God did yesterday in the Sunday morning service. You can discuss the spiritual results that came from the preaching and ministry of your church, reflecting on the ways God is at work in the lives of other people. These types of conversations can occur any time of the week and are often casual, friendly, and very exciting. Additional conversations could be with friends who are passionate about similar areas of ministry that you have. You could spend time discussing what more could be done to best minister to your area of focus in your congregation. You could rehearse what produced spiritual growth in the past and what can be done to continue to solidify spiritual decisions made. Make a conscience effort to remember to praise God for all He has done and is doing in the lives of people.

Lastly, take some time to begin brief, friendly conversations with Christians in your church, workplace, and home. Ask:

"What is exciting about what God is doing in your life?"

"Is He teaching you anything this month about Himself?"

"Has God given you guidance regarding any decisions you were praying to Him about in this last month?"

"Have you had (or heard of) any prayer requests that God has specifically answered in the last few weeks?"

"If God has answered any prayers recently, how did He answer t he request?"

"Did He answer in the way you thought He would?"

Of course, after every question, ask yourself:

"How can all that I am talking about and hearing about apply to me?"

"How can I take what I have just heard testified about God's guidance, power, and goodness and inculcate it into my heart, life and practice?"

It is important to continue this practice of having intentional, spiritual discussion with other believers. It is this rehearsing of spiritual truth that revives our soul, informs our worship, and makes our minds not only well-versed in the Scriptures, but it also encourages our hearts to crave spiritual things. If you string enough spiritual discussions together, you will find that you do not want to go a day without engaging other believers in these types of discussions.

WALK IN SERVICE

This section would be a great springboard for group discussion. It contains a lot of points that tend to be of interest to many believers. We only wish we could attend some of your discussion groups as you process these spiritual teachings. Here are some leading questions we encourage you to discuss:

1. According to our description in chapter 10, how would you answer this question, "What is a godly person?"

2. What was your initial thought when you read that there is a difference between a mere Christian and a godly Christian? Possibly consider Galatians 6:1 where it describes how believers ought to not only keep a fallen believer accountable, but also to restore him/her "in a spirit of gentleness."

3. What is your opinion of the definition of a godly person being one who is self-disciplined in godly attitudes and habits?

4. Have everyone in the group prayerfully consider if they are indeed a godly person, according to the description that's been established. Have a time of prayer so that your discussion group members can ask the Lord to forgive them and/or thank Him for His power to become a godly person once again.

5. Read Psalm 139 together as a group. Take time to stop and pause at the end of each section to reflect on the details of God's immutable attributes (omniscience, omnipresence, and omnipotence). Spend one session on each division of this Psalm to ponder the vastness of the greatness of our God. Then take time to comprehend the great care that the Psalmist took to tell God that he wanted to be looked upon as different from anyone who finds it easy to blaspheme the Lord. Ask yourself if you do all you can do to make sure that you are far removed from anything that would cause people to think that you do not honor the Lord Jesus Christ. Think of little things you could do that would make a tactful statement to all that you are indeed different.

6. Consider the teaching of John 14:1-3. Ask the very simple question, "Am I a faithful bride?" Depending on the group dynamic, this

self-assessment could be done privately, or it could be a time to share your victories and your struggles with one another. This question could go two ways in your life. We would encourage you to identify what you believe you are doing that the Lord is indeed pleased with. We know this may be somewhat uncomfortable for some because you actually will be articulating things that you believe you are doing right before the Lord. But don't feel that you are being prideful or arrogant. You could preface your statements with these words, "Lord, thank You for giving me the wisdom to see what I need to do. Keep me close to You and I will strive to remain obedient to You." Remember, as a Father, our Lord longs to observe the obedience of His children, and He longs to bless His children immensely. Also, identify what areas of your life you could improve on so that you are always living as a faithful bride. As you do this, pray to the Lord – the One who both loves you and desires the absolute best for you – and tell Him why you think you have been tempted to disobey Him in specific areas of your life. Confess to Him that you are sorry and that you regret giving in to those passions. Then, begin to tell Him what you will do for the remainder of the day to safeguard your heart and mind from considering being unfaithful to Him.

As you enter into these group discussions, don't try to gain spiritual victory in one all-encompassing action or activity. You did not just fall into sin all of a sudden, nor will the recovery back to a strong state require only one magical action or activity. You need to take baby steps in your spiritual walk – one day at a time, one moment at a time. Create little and numerous spiritual victories in your life. Take time to praise the Lord and celebrate these times of obedience by talking with a friend and let them know that, "Hey, I made it through another day!" Or, "We had a good time focusing on spiritual things tonight, and my mind was focused more than it has been in a long time."

Make a list or keep a journal of what seem to be "little spiritual victories" that you could celebrate and praise the Lord for. Consider if there are daily victories, half-day victories, even hourly victories. We believe this ability of seeing progress and experiencing victories will encourage you not to throw away all that the Spirit has done and is obviously doing in your life to keep you faithful to Him!

TALK ABOUT YOUR WALK

Building on what we practiced earlier, begin now to prepare for a longer presentation of the gospel message, one that lasts 4-7 minutes. Take what you have learned in Chapter Seven and begin to work on a well-framed, systematic, well-thought-out presentation of these spiritual truths. Prepare a presentation for a receptive seeker who is willing to listen. Be prepared for questions that may not relate to what you are trying to share. Also be prepared for someone who may have a hostile reaction and wants to argue. Remember, confidence in God and a well-prepared presentation will dispel fear.

Take a moment to think of someone specifically who is in need of hearing the gospel message. Begin praying for this person by name. Tell the Lord how you feel about this person and why you chose his/her name. Tell the Lord how you feel about sharing these truths with him/her. Are you scared? Nervous? Excited? Impatient? Happy? Sad? Then articulate to God exactly why you feel this way. Rehearse the teachings that you have learned, and see if any of these verses provide the knowledge that you need in order to overcome your fears. Rehearse in your mind what the Bible teaches regarding what salvation is and is not. These are methods to be prepared in many ways as you share the truths of the gospel message with others.

So, the only remaining fear is possibly, "What if they ask me a question that is not addressed in this book?" Then your answer is, "Well, good question. I don't know the answer right now, but if you would allow me a little time, I'll ask someone who may know and/or find a resource that answers your question.

Then I'll get back with you." Remember, unless you are a scholar with a Ph.D. in every academic field of discipline, you are bound to say, "I don't know" a few million times in your lifetime. There is no shame in not knowing how to respond immediately.

Simply write down the question, or make a list if they have several questions, and then tell them that you will research the answer and get back to them. But be quick to ask them a question in return, "If I take the time to research the issue, and I return to you with a response that supports the Bible and its teaching about salvation, will you then believe that the Bible is true and give your heart to Jesus Christ?" Of course, if someone is not sincere, they will shrug this off and give other excuses as to why they do not believe – and that shows you that regardless, their heart is set on not believing in Jesus Christ. But the sincere ones will realize that they will be put to a point of decision if you return with sound answers to their questions.

Remember also that when you are witnessing and being kind and respectful, you are not the only one who has to answer questions. It is also incumbent upon the one to whom you are witnessing to respond to your questions as well. So ask them a lot of questions. Make them tell you what they believe about salvation. Ask them follow up questions like, "So, according to your way, I could work for my own salvation. So, how do I know when I have done enough good things? Who makes this judgment call? Do other imperfect humans decide this?" Or you could use a line of questioning like, "If peace is found within ourselves, how do we know that we are always right and guiding ourselves down a healthy path? Do I know if my path is perfect until I become perfect and all-knowing? Has anyone ever reached that goal of perfection? If so, should we then begin to consult him/her?" Ask questions of the ones you are witnessing to and listen to them. Then after you have asked them questions and listened to them, ask them more questions about their beliefs and listen some more. You may find that the more they rehearse their belief system, the more they realize the gaping holes in it.

Throughout this book, we have asked you to consider many crucial topics that are significant in making wise decisions—big decisions and small decisions that could have life-long consequences. We discussed the important role of critical thinking, and we identified an assortment of flawed arguments. We believe your ability to identify these fallacies can help you make better choices. We asked you to consider the idea that it is through the process of critical thinking that life's most important decisions can be made and major mistakes can be avoided.

We have equipped you with descriptions of the philosophies of various worldviews and have asked you to consider how your worldview impacts every area of your life. If you have yet to determine your worldview, we urge you to seek out truth in the Word of God.

We have covered the basic tenets in the message of Christianity—spiritual truths that are included in the gospel message concerning Jesus Christ. If you embrace the Biblical/Christian worldview, we have encouraged you to be prepared—with knowledge of the truth, with a heart of compassion and with an abundance of patience.

LIFE IS TOO SHORT

It has been said, "Practice does not make perfect. Practice only makes permanent. Perfect practice makes perfect." The spiritual activities presented in this final chapter are for the purpose of spurring you on to practice what you have learned in this book. Of course, there are many more activities and ideas that would help you solidify these teachings in your heart. So, we encourage you to think of more ways – unique ways – that you believe would honor the Lord, protect the pure gospel message, and be effective in reaching others with the saving knowledge of Jesus Christ. Our deepest heart's cry for you as a believer in Jesus Christ is for you to know the Lord more intimately, testify of His saving grace, love, and mercy to those around you, and for you to be a walking example of holiness, righteousness, and purity before those who are observing you and looking up to you for a spiritual example by which to model their own lives.

Life is too short and God's truth too precious to keep His message contained within us or to squander our testimony by pursuing sin. Even though our hearts desire is to join each and every one of you at your churches, ministries, and missions, and to worship with you in rehearsing these wonderful truths together, our only request is that you make a lifetime commitment to purpose in your heart to live out the following words of the Apostle Paul:

> Dear friends, you always followed my instructions when I was with you. And now that I am away, it is even more important. Work hard to show the results of your salvation, obeying God with deep reverence and fear. For God is working in you, giving you the desire and the power to do what pleases him. (Philippians 2:12-13, NLT)

In these last few chapters, we have emphasized an essential component of sharing our faith with others. We must earn a hearing. We must walk our talk. Before we attempt to share the truth of the gospel, representing the God of the Bible—we first must examine our own hearts. We have two final questions for you to consider:

1. Are you certain that you have a Biblical/Christian Worldview?
2. Has your heart been eternally changed by the One who granted you eternal life through His name, Jesus Christ?

ABOUT THE AUTHORS

Dr. Lew Weider is Director of the Center for Christian/Community Service at Liberty University. He is also Professor of Contemporary Issues and has been teaching at Liberty since 1985. He also serves as an Associate Pastor and Deacon of Thomas Road Baptist Church. Dr. Weider received a Bachelor of Science in Religion and a Master of Arts in Christian Thought from Liberty University, and an Ed.D in Higher Education from Argosy University in Sarasota, Florida. He teaches weekly at the Thomas Road Baptist Church. He is the author of Contemporary Issues I: AFirming a Biblical Worldview, 3rd edition (2010) and Contemporary Issues II: Applying a Biblical Worldview, 3rd edition (2010), both published by Academx. He is also a contributor to the Popular Encyclopedia of Apologetics (2008) published by Harvest House.

Dr. Weider and his wife Cheryl have two grown daughters, Crystal Beams and Michelle, and they reside in Lynchburg, Virginia.

Dr. Ben Gutierrez is Professor of Religion at Liberty University in Lynchburg, Virginia. He also serves as an Associate Pastor of Thomas Road Baptist Church. Dr. Gutierrez received a Diploma from Word of Life Bible Institute, and AA and BS in Religion from Liberty University, a Master of Arts in Religion and a Master of Divinity from Liberty Baptist Theological Seminary, and PhD from Regent University. He is the author of, Living out the Mind of Christ: Practical Keys to Discovering and Applying the Mind of Christ in Everyday Life – a recommended Innovate Church resource for all pastors and Christian leaders. He is also the co-author of Learn to Read New Testament Greek Workbook (2009) published by Broadman and Holman, an excellent resource to supplement one's study of the Koine Greek language; and Ministry Is: How to serve Jesus with Passion and Confidence (2010) published by Broadman and Holman, a practical guide on how to serve effectively in the local church.

Dr. Gutierrez and his wife Tammy have two daughters, Lauren and Emma, and reside in Lynchburg, Virginia.